# My Amazing BODY MACHINE

DK

# ROBERT WINSTON

# My Amazing
# BODY
# MACHINE

Illustrated by *Owen Gildersleeve*

**Written by** Richard Walker
**Illustrated by** Owen Gildersleeve
**Senior editors** Marie Greenwood,
Ruth O'Rourke
**Senior designer** Jim Green
**US Senior editor** Shannon Beatty
**Design assistant** Rhea Gaughan
**Additional illustrations** Molly Lattin
**Pre-production** Nadine King
**Production** Srijana Gurung,
Niamh Tierney
**Managing editor** Laura Gilbert
**Managing art editor** Diane Peyton Jones
**Art director** Martin Wilson
**Publisher** Sarah Larter
**Publishing director** Sophie Mitchell

First American Edition, 2017
Published in the United States by DK Publishing
345 Hudson Street, New York, New York 10014

Copyright © 2017 Dorling Kindersley Limited
DK, a Division of Penguin Random House LLC
18 19 20 21  10 9 8 7 6 5 4
008-298811-June/2017

A catalog record for this book is available from
the Library of Congress.

ISBN 978-1-4654-6185-8

DK books are available at special discounts when purchased
in bulk for sales promotions, premiums, fund-raising, or
educational use. For details, contact: DK Publishing Special
Markets, 345 Hudson Street, New York, New York 10014
SpecialSales@dk.com

Printed and bound in China

A WORLD OF IDEAS:
SEE ALL THERE IS TO KNOW

www.dk.com

# Contents

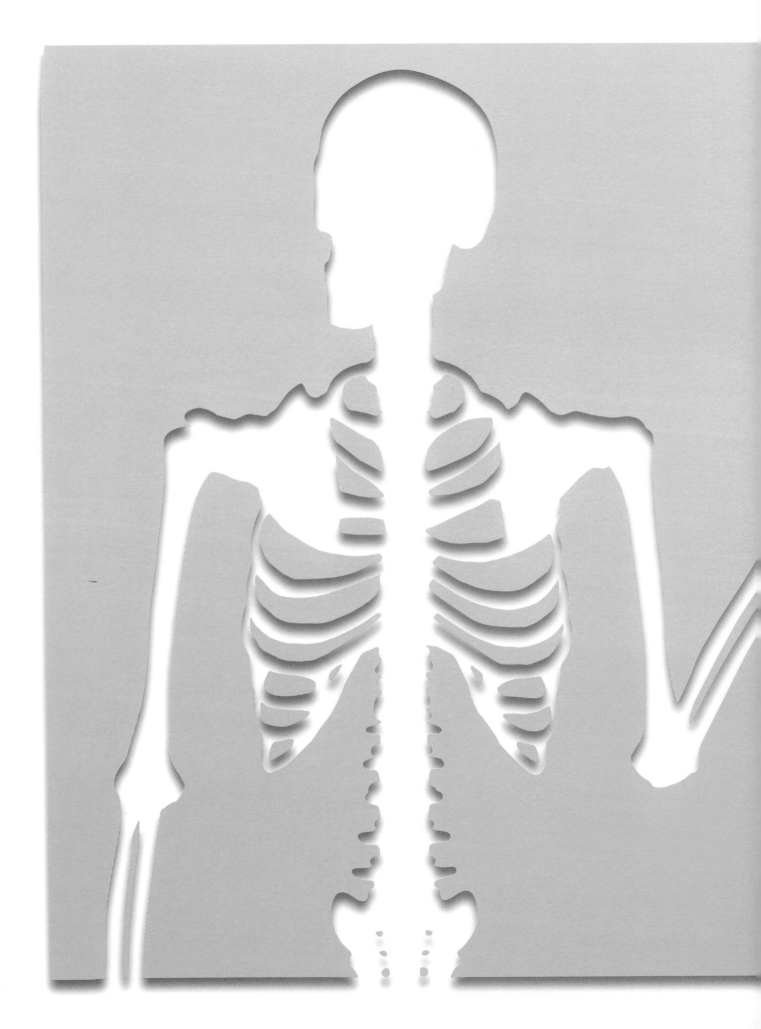

# Foreword

You own a most powerful and intricate machine. No skilled engineer or craftsman anywhere can make anything as complex or precious. This machine is your own body. And unlike other machines, it can make the most delicate and complicated movements, and it can feel, think, and love. And, remarkably, it grows.

This machine of yours is controlled by the brain, the most complicated structure known, far more powerful than the most advanced computer. And each person's brain is unique—making each one of us special. In that body is your heart, a pump only the size of an orange, but pumping around 10½ pints (five liters) of fluid each minute, day after day, usually for over 70 years without needing repair. No mechanic can manufacture anything as effective.

This book is about these and other organs in your body machine. All of them have amazed me ever since I went to school. Look after your special machine carefully; it is so very precious.

Robert Winston.

# Building the Machine

It takes trillions and trillions of tiny living parts, called cells, to build just one amazing body machine. Guided by detailed instructions, these cells are organized into bigger parts that work together to make you, a unique human being.

# Code of life

Every one of your cells contain the instructions needed to build and run your body machine. These instructions are called genes. Genes are found in tiny strands called chromosomes. There are 46 chromosomes in the control center, or nucleus, of each cell.

You and other humans share about **50 percent** of your DNA with **bananas!**

## Building instructions

Chromosomes are made from a tightly wound string of a substance called DNA. Each piece of DNA has two strands that wind around each other. This is called a double helix. Four different bases join the two strands. In this illustration, each base has a different color.

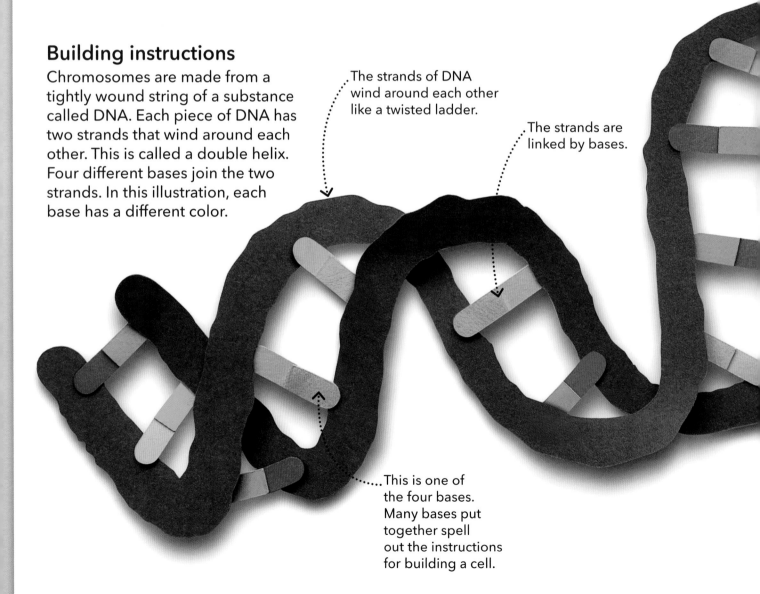

The strands of DNA wind around each other like a twisted ladder.

The strands are linked by bases.

This is one of the four bases. Many bases put together spell out the instructions for building a cell.

## Boy or girl?

Every cell has 23 pairs of chromosomes. One pair, called the sex chromosomes, controls whether someone is male or female. Boys have one X ( pink) and one Y (blue) chromosome, as shown here. Girls have two X chromosomes, and no Y.

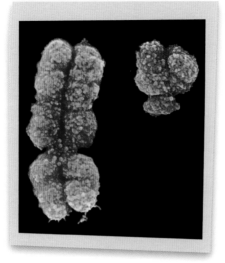

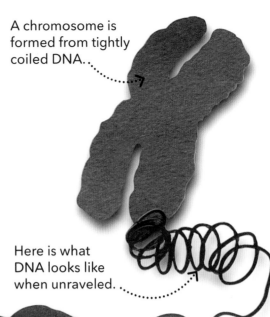

A chromosome is formed from tightly coiled DNA.

Here is what DNA looks like when unraveled.

Green bases stick to red bases, and yellow bases stick to blue.

If unraveled, the DNA in each cell would measure about 7 ft (2.1 m) long.

## Two of a kind

These girls are identical twins. They look just like each other because they share exactly the same genes. However, each girl will live her own life and different things will happen to her, so she will develop her own unique personality.

# One of a kind

Every one of your body's cells contains a set of instructions. Those instructions, called genes, are used to build your body and make you look human. They also give you a unique mix of features that makes you one of a kind.

The shape of your mouth ......

......Your skin color

......Whether or not you have freckles

## Genes and inheritance

The way you look largely depends on your genes. You inherit these genes from your parents. There are slightly different versions of some genes. One might give you brown eyes, for example, while another would give you blue eyes. It is your particular mix of genes that makes you unique. Hereare some features that are controlled by the genes you inherit.

The color of your eyes ......

Whether you can roll your tongue ......

Your hair color ......

Whether you are
a girl or a boy

Whether your hair
is curly or straight

The features
and proportions
of your face

Whether your earlobes are
free or attached to the side
of your face

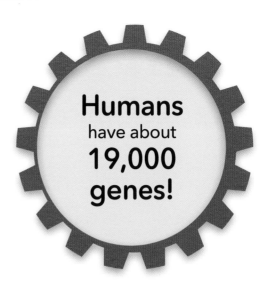

**Humans**
have about
**19,000
genes!**

## Passing it on

This is an example of how genes are passed on.
Both parents have different versions of an eye-color
gene. A child receives one version from each parent.
If the child inherits one or two brown-eye genes,
they will have brown eyes. The child has to inherit
two blue-eye genes to have blue eyes.

Although the dad has
brown eyes, he also
has the blue-eye gene.

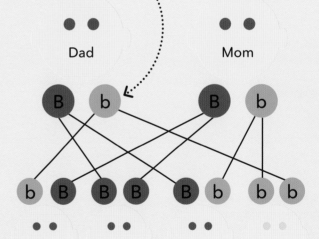

Dad                           Mom

Children

The brown-eye gene
always beats the
blue-eye gene, so this
child has brown eyes.

A child will only
have blue eyes
if they have two
blue-eye genes.

# Mini-machine

Your body is made up of trillions and trillions of tiny parts called cells. Cells come in many different shapes and they all have a different job to do. Every cell is like a tiny machine. It has many different parts, called organelles, that work together.

Bags that carry waste and water inside the cell are called vacuoles.

The nucleus is the cell's control center.

Little bags of fluid, called lysosomes, digest food and eat up waste or worn-out organelles inside the cell.

The Golgi body is an organelle that takes proteins made inside the cell and sends them to where they are needed.

The cell is filled with clear jelly called cytoplasm.

## Inside a cell

Look inside this cell to see its many tiny working parts. In the middle is the control center, called the nucleus. This sends instructions to the cell to keep it running smoothly.

A network of tubes and bags carry material through the cell.

These tubes help build things called proteins that your body needs to work properly.

Muscle tissue is made of stringy cells, called fibers. It makes you move.

Nerve tissue carries messages around your body.

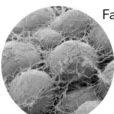
Fat tissue sits under your skin. Its round cells store energy and keep you warm.

Blood is a liquid tissue. Its red blood cells carry oxygen to other tissues.

## Join together

A group of similar cells that come together to do a particular job is called a tissue. These include muscle, nerve, fat, and blood tissues.

Tiny batteries, called mitochondria, power the cell.

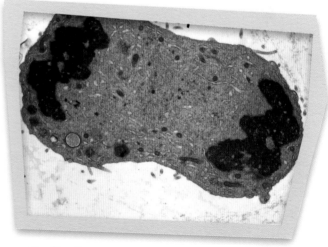

More than **2,000 dead skin cells** fell off you as you read this sentence!

## Splitting up

Cells split in half to make new ones. The half-sized cells then grow to full size. You started life as a single cell, which divided again and again to make the trillions of cells in your body. Your cells divide all the time to replace worn-out ones.

# Getting organized

The living cells that make up your body do not work on their own. Cells with the same job form teams called tissues. Different tissues get together to make working parts called organs, such as the brain and stomach.

## Body systems

Organs that are linked together, such as the heart and blood vessels, make a body system. Your body has 12 systems, and 10 are shown here. The other two are the skin and the reproductive system. Systems need one another to make the body work properly.

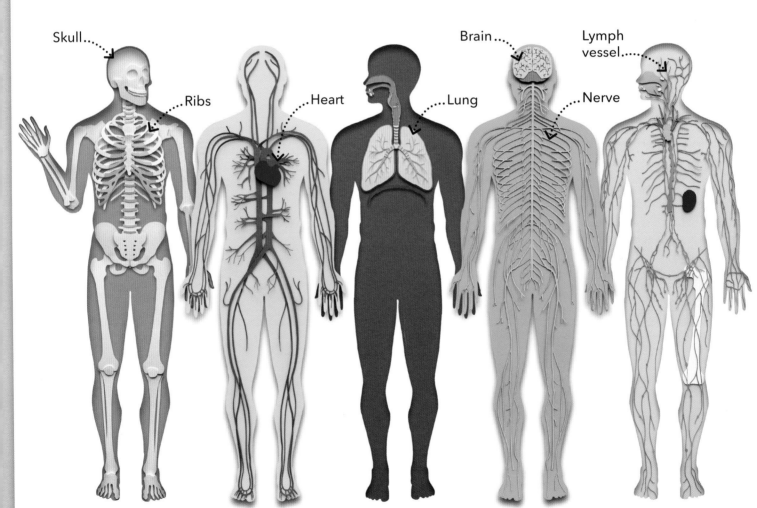

Skull........

........Ribs

Brain.....

Lymph vessel.......

......Heart

.......Lung

........Nerve

**Skeletal system**
Your skeleton supports the body, allows it to move, and protects organs.

**Circulatory system**
Pumped by the heart, blood carries food and oxygen in blood vessels.

**Respiratory system**
This breathes in air to get the oxygen that is used by body cells.

**Nervous system**
The brain controls your body. It sends and gets messages along nerves.

**Lymphatic and immune systems**
Lymph vessels drain fluid from tissues. Defense cells destroy germs.

# Working parts

There are more than 2,000 working parts, called organs, in your body. Every organ has a particular job or jobs to do. Your brain, for example, controls your body, and lets you feel and see, think and remember. Your stomach plays a key part in breaking down the food that you eat.

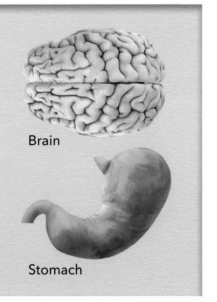

Brain

Stomach

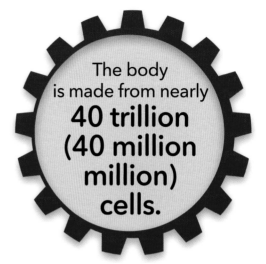

The body is made from nearly **40 trillion (40 million million) cells.**

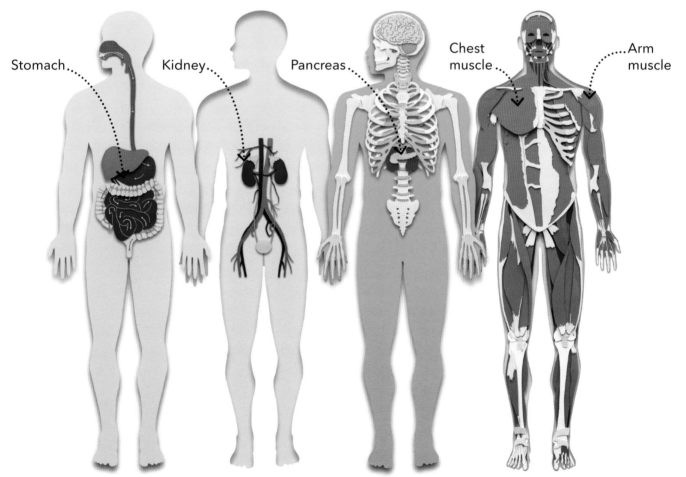

Stomach

Kidney

Pancreas

Chest muscle

Arm muscle

**Digestive system**
This digests food to release nutrients needed for energy, growth, and repair.

**Urinary system**
The kidneys filter blood. Waste and excess water leave the body as urine.

**Endocrine system**
These glands release chemical messengers, called hormones.

**Muscular system**
Muscles tighten, or contract, to pull bones so your body can move.

# Body barrier

The skin is your body's biggest organ. It makes a barrier that covers and protects you. It keeps out germs, helps to regulate your temperature, and lets you feel your surroundings. It also helps protect you from the sun's harmful rays and constantly repairs itself.

## Living layers

Your skin has two layers. A thin top layer called the epidermis provides protection and is constantly worn away and replaced. The inner layer is called the dermis. It contains blood vessels, nerves, and sweat glands that help the skin carry out its work, and provides the cells which grow up into the top layer.

The top of the epidermis gets worn away as skin flakes.

Oily sebum coats a hair.

Tiny blood vessels, called capillaries, lie near the skin's surface.

Nerve endings detect touch, heat, or pain.

This is a gland that releases an oily mixture called sebum. It softens skin and hair.

Hair grows out of a little pocket called a follicle.

Nerves carry signals to the brain.

The hair grows upward from the follicle.

## Hair

This close-up picture shows two of the thousands of hairs that cover your head. Each hair is a flexible strand made up of dead cells. Hairs protect the skin on the head from harmful sun rays.

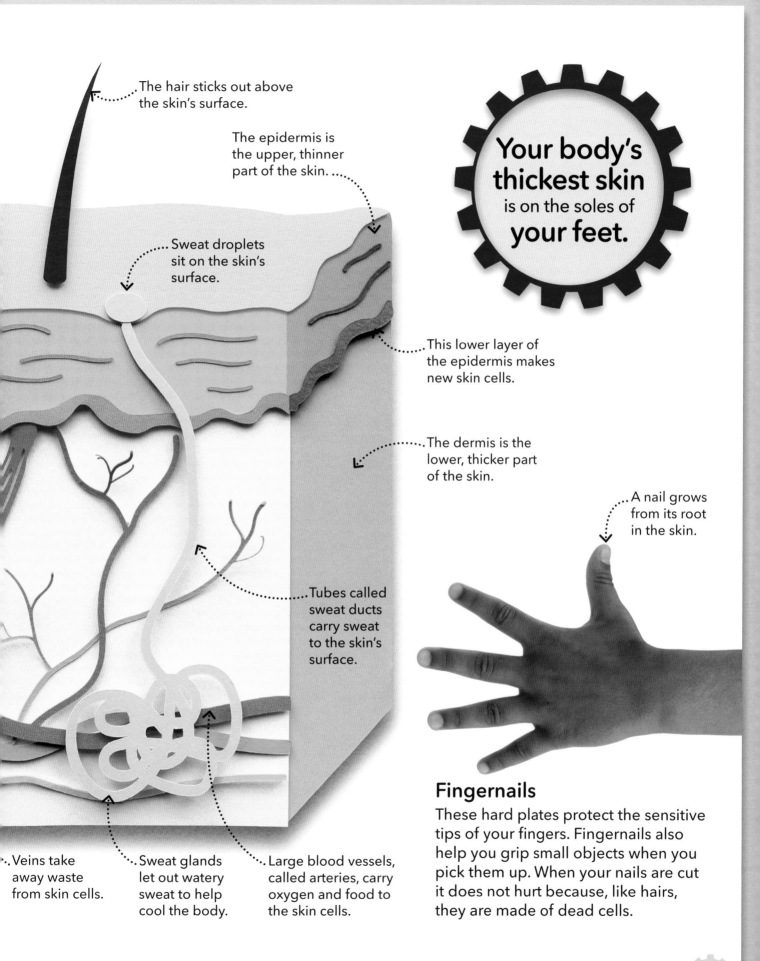

The hair sticks out above the skin's surface.

The epidermis is the upper, thinner part of the skin.

Sweat droplets sit on the skin's surface.

This lower layer of the epidermis makes new skin cells.

The dermis is the lower, thicker part of the skin.

Tubes called sweat ducts carry sweat to the skin's surface.

Veins take away waste from skin cells.

Sweat glands let out watery sweat to help cool the body.

Large blood vessels, called arteries, carry oxygen and food to the skin cells.

**Your body's thickest skin** is on the soles of **your feet.**

A nail grows from its root in the skin.

## Fingernails

These hard plates protect the sensitive tips of your fingers. Fingernails also help you grip small objects when you pick them up. When your nails are cut it does not hurt because, like hairs, they are made of dead cells.

# Marvelous machine

Your body's cells, tissues, organs, and systems do not work separately. To create and run the marvelous machine that is you, they work together and support one another every second of the day.

## Body parts

Your body has thousands of parts that have their own jobs to do. They also work together to keep the body alive and make it work efficiently. Here are some of your main body parts.

Your brain lets you move, see, feel, think, create, and remember. Along with the rest of the nervous system, it also controls breathing and most other body activities.

A gland in your neck, called the thyroid gland, is part of the endocrine system. It releases chemical messengers, called hormones, which help to control your growth and energy.

Your lymph vessels and glands collect fluid from your tissues, filter it, then pick out and destroy the germs that cause disease.

These arteries (red) and veins (blue) are part of the circulatory system that carries blood around your body.

Your lungs suck in air and pass oxygen from it into your blood. Oxygen is carried to your cells and releases the energy that keeps you alive.

The intestines are part of your digestive system, which breaks down food into tiny pieces that your cells can use for energy, growth, and repair.

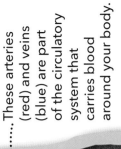
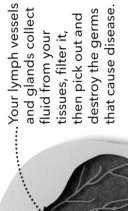
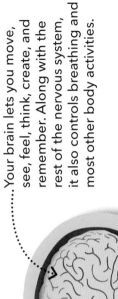

Bones form the skeletal system, the slightly flexible framework that supports your body and allows it to move. The skeleton protects soft organs.

Muscles pull on bones and move your skeleton when instructed to by the brain. This allows you to walk, jump, or wave. Muscles also help shape your body.

**Water,** the most important substance in your body, makes up **over half** of your weight.

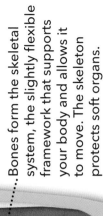

The skin is a tough, waterproof layer that covers your body and protects it from germs, injury, and sunlight. It also helps keep your insides warm.

## Build a body

Your body is built from basic substances called elements. The most common ones are oxygen, carbon, hydrogen, nitrogen, calcium, and phosphorus. Other elements include sodium, chlorine, and iron. Elements often combine. For example, oxygen and hydrogen combine to make water.

Nitrogen, found in air, helps to make body-building proteins.

Phosphorus, also found in match tips, makes teeth and bones strong.

Iron, also found in nails, helps make blood red and carry oxygen.

Carbon, also found in diamonds, builds big molecules inside you.

Calcium, also found in chalk, helps build bones and keeps muscles working.

Sodium and chlorine combine to make salt, a key part of blood.

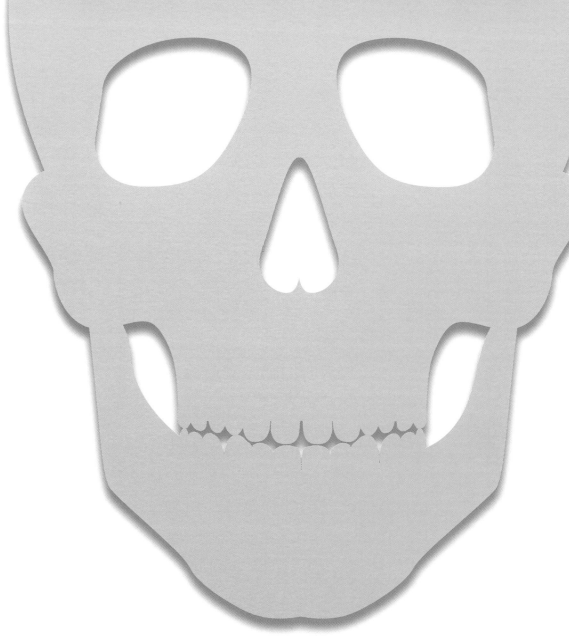

Super
Structures

Without strong bones and powerful muscles, your body would collapse in a heap. Together, these super structures shape and support your body, protect your insides, and allow you to perform all kinds of movements, from smiling to kicking a ball.

# Framework

Without a skeleton, your body would collapse in a heap! This flexible framework supports and shapes your body, and allows it to move. Your skeleton also protects your organs.

## Skeleton bones

Your skeleton's bones are connected by joints that let your body move around. More than half of your bones are in your hands and feet. These bones help you perform complex movements, such as gripping a pen.

Your skull protects your brain and gives shape to your face.

Your jaw is hinged near your ears. It allows the lower jawbone to move up and down, so that you can talk and eat.

Your shoulder blade (scapula) is a flat triangle of bone that makes a joint with your upper arm bone in the shoulder.

Twelve pairs of curved bones, called ribs, make a cage. Your rib cage protects the organs in your chest.

Your upper and lower arm bones meet at your elbow joint.

The hip bones (pelvis) support organs and form joints with the thighbones.

These bones, separated by bendy cartilage, form the spine, which supports the upper body

There are **206 bones** in an adult skeleton, but you were born with more than **300.**

Your fingers are each made up of three connected bones. These are called phalanges.

Your kneecap (patella) sits at the front of your knee. It helps the thigh muscles to straighten your leg

Your shinbone (tibia) joins your knee to your ankle. You can feel its sharp edge at the front of your shin.

The ankle joint, which lets you bend your foot, is formed where the two lower leg bones meet the ankle bone in your foot.

There are 26 bones in each foot.

Your thighbone (femur) connects the hip (pelvis) to your knee. It is the longest bone in the body.

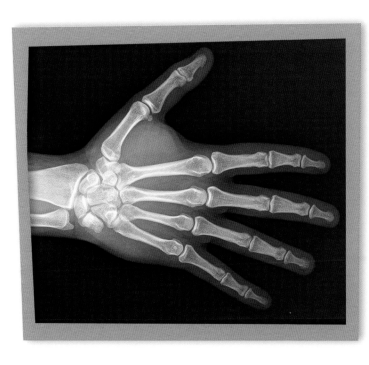

## Look inside

You can feel your bones under your skin, but to see them you need to use a special type of camera, called an X-ray machine. Bones, such as these hand bones, show up very clearly in X-rays, so doctors use them to check for broken bones.

25

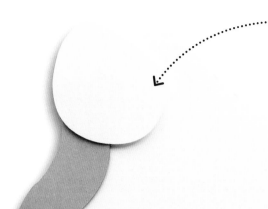

The wider end, or head, of the bone is made mainly of spongy bone. The head forms a joint with another bone.

## Inside a bone

The outer layer of compact bone makes a bone, such as this thighbone, hard. It surrounds spongy bone that, despite its name, is not squishy but light and strong. Jellylike bone marrow fills the middle of many bones.

The shaft of a long bone connects its two heads. It is made mostly of compact bone and bone marrow.

# Bone structure

If your bones were solid, you would be too heavy to move. But if you cut open a bone, you would see that there are both solid parts and spaces. All bones share the same special structure. They are light enough not to weigh you down, but strong enough to support your body.

## Blood factory

Here is a close-up view of bone marrow, a tissue that is found inside many bones. Bone marrow makes new blood cells. These replace older ones that are worn out. The red dots in this picture are red blood cells.

Spongy bone

Metal arch

# Super structures

Spongy bone gets its strength from its honeycomb-like structure of bars, or struts, that cross over each other. This criss-cross pattern has been copied in buildings and structures, such as this arch.

Compact bone covers the outer part of the bone. It is made of tiny rods that give it strength and hardness.

Bone marrow, which fills the center of the bone, makes blood cells that enter the blood.

The spaces in spongy bone also contain bone marrow.

The tough "skin" that protects a bone is called the periosteum. It helps, along with the tendons, to connect the bone to the muscles that move it.

Your bone marrow makes **two million** red blood cells every second.

Spongy bone fills most of the head of the bone. It has lots of little hollows that make the bone lighter.

# Growing and healing

Bones are living organs that contain blood vessels, nerves, and bone cells. They first appear when a baby is inside its mother, and continue growing until about the age of 20. Bones can repair themselves if they break.

## Growing bones

At first, a baby's bones are made from a tough but flexible material called cartilage. As the bones grow, the cartilage is replaced by harder bone. As you can see from these X-rays, cartilage continues to be replaced by bone as the child grows.

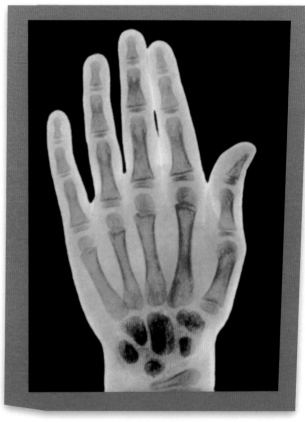

**Seven-year-old child**
Here, the wristbones, and the bones of the palm and the fingers, are steadily growing as cartilage is replaced by bone.

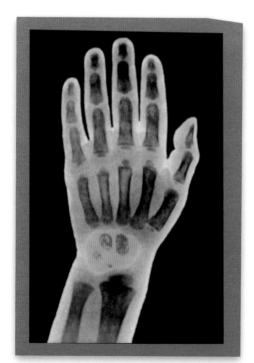

**Two-year-old child**
Here, the wristbones (pink) are made mostly from cartilage.

The **bones broken most commonly** are in the fingers, wrists, and ankles.

## Auto-repair

Although bones are strong, they sometimes break or crack. If this happens, a bone starts to repair itself right away. Within months it will be almost like new. Sometimes, casts or pins are used to hold bones together so they heal properly.

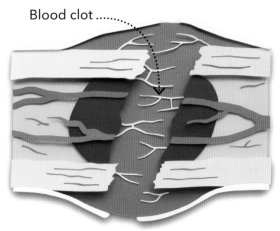

Blood clot ......

**One to two hours**
A blood clot forms between the ends of the broken bone to stop bleeding. White blood cells arrive to mop up any invading germs.

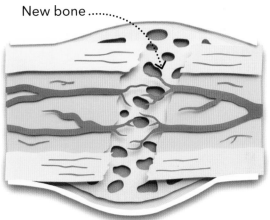

New bone ........

**Three weeks**
Bone-building cells move into the space between the broken ends and build a "bridge" of spongy bone. The bone cannot yet support weight.

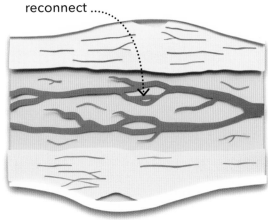

Blood vessels reconnect ......

**Three months**
The bone is repaired. The spongy bone "bridge" has been replaced by hard compact bone. Blood vessels in the bone marrow connect together across the break.

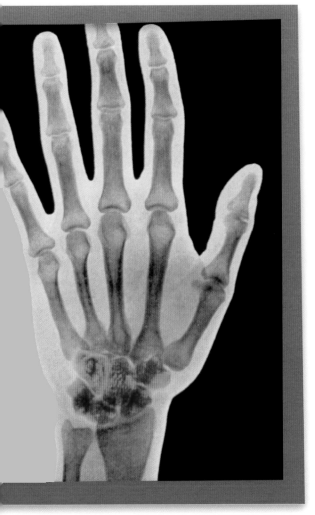

**Adult hand**
This adult hand has eight wrist bones, along with the fully grown palm and finger bones.

# Skull and spine

Both your skull and your spine, or backbone, form an important part of your skeleton. Your skull protects your brain and sense organs and shapes how you look. It sits on top of your spine, the flexible column that holds your body upright.

There are **29 bones in your head,** including six tiny ear bones that help you hear.

The frontal bone shapes your forehead and is one of the bones that protects your brain.

An eye socket, or orbit, surrounds and protects each eye. It is formed from seven skull bones.

## Brain box

Your skull is made of 22 bones. All bones, apart from the lower jawbone, are locked together. This makes your skull super strong. Eight skull bones form the domed box that surrounds and protects your brain. The other 14 bones shape your face and hold your teeth.

The cheekbone, or zygomatic bone, is part of your eye socket.

Your nose is mostly cartilage.

The lower jaw is the only skull bone that moves. It lets you eat, drink, breathe, and speak.

Seven neck, or cervical, vertebrae support your head. They let it nod, shake, and turn. ........

A disk made of pliable cartilage sits in between each pair of vertebrae. ....

Twelve chest, or thoracic, vertebrae form joints with your ribs, the curved bones that shape your chest. ....

In your lower back are five large lumbar vertebrae. These bones support most of your body's weight. ...

The sacrum, made of five bones stuck together, anchors your hips, or pelvis, to the rest of the spine. ..

You have a tail, but it is inside your body! The tailbone, or coccyx, is made of four small bones that are stuck together. ..

## Flexible backbone

Your S-shaped spine is a chain of many odd-shaped bones called vertebrae. There is a small amount of flexibility between each pair of vertebrae. Added together, these small movements make the whole spine very flexible, allowing it to bend and twist.

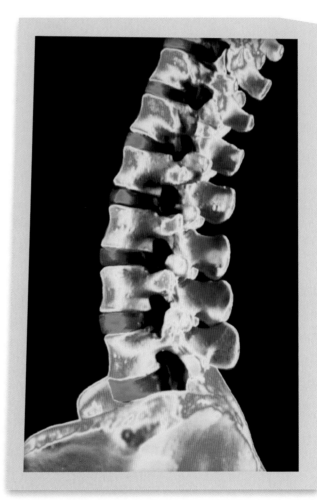

## Shock absorber

This X-ray shows the cartilage disks (blue/green) that are sandwiched between vertebrae. These disks are tough but springy. When you run or jump, the disks squash slightly to cushion you from any harsh jolts.

# Moving parts

Joints are where your bones meet. Although some are fixed solidly, most of your joints move freely. Without them your body would be stiff and rigid, making walking, running, waving your arms, or wiggling your toes impossible.

## Types of joint

You have several types of free-moving joints in your body. Each type allows certain body parts a range of movements. The type of movement depends on how bone ends fit together in the joint.

Your shoulder's ball-and-socket joint allows the arm to move freely in most directions. There is also one at the top of each leg.

In the joint in the wrist, the curved ends of two bones fit together. It allows the hand to move up and down and from side to side.

In this pivot joint, at the top of the spine, an upper bone turns around the lower bone. This allows the head to shake from side to side.

A flexible joint in the thumb can tilt in any direction, but not twist.

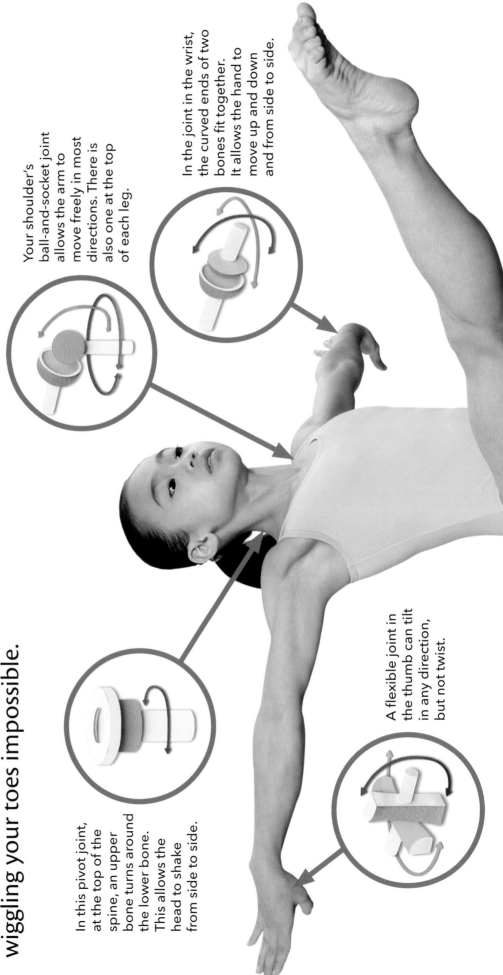

The hinge joint in the knee works like a door hinge and can only move backward or forward to let the knee bend or straighten.

In the ankle, joints let the flat ends of two bones slide against each other. These allow small gliding movements that help to support the foot.

The **smallest** joints are the synovial joints in **the ear,** between tiny bones that help you hear.

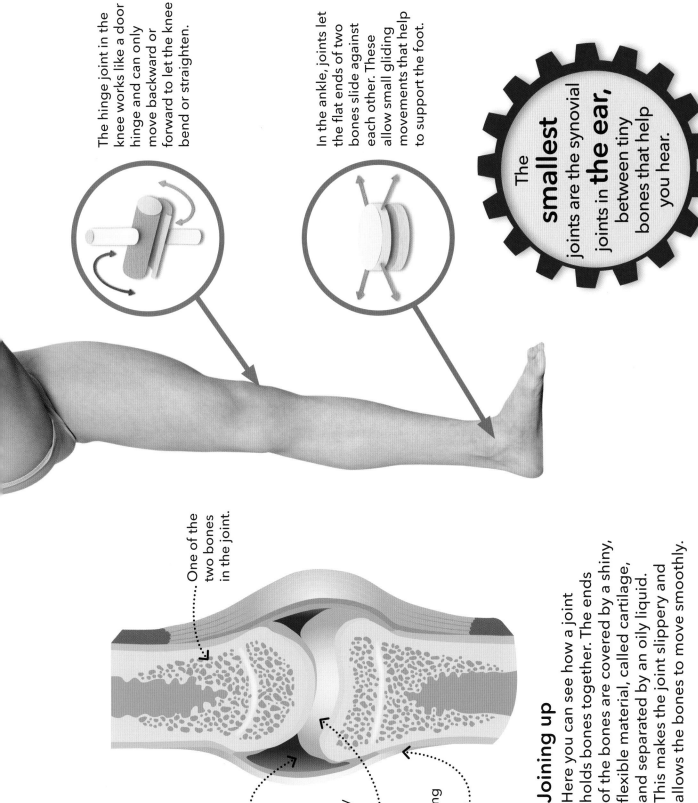

One of the two bones in the joint.

An oily fluid fills the space between bones.

Smooth, slippery cartilage covers the bone ends.

Bones are held together by strong bands of tissue, called ligaments.

## Joining up

Here you can see how a joint holds bones together. The ends of the bones are covered by a shiny, flexible material, called cartilage, and separated by an oily liquid. This makes the joint slippery and allows the bones to move smoothly.

# Moving machine

Whether walking, talking, or smiling, your body machine is constantly on the move. Muscles make those moves happen. Using fuel from food, muscles get shorter, or contract, to pull your bones. Other muscles pump your blood or help you eat and breathe.

## Body muscles

The muscles that move your skeleton are found in layers under your skin. Here you can see surface muscles on the left and deeper muscles on the right. Some are named, along with the movements they produce. More than 640 skeletal muscles shape your body and make up half of your weight. Muscles are connected to your bones by tendons.

The frontalis wrinkles your forehead and raises your eyebrows when you are surprised.

This muscle surrounding the mouth closes your lips and pushes them outward, such as during kissing.

This chest muscle bends and pulls your arm forward and toward your body, and turns it inward.

The deltoid raises your arm away from your body to the front, side, or backward.

The external oblique twists your upper body and bends it forward or sideways.

This forearm muscle bends the fingers.

The biceps muscle pulls a bone in your forearm to bend the arm at the elbow.

This muscle pulls your leg inward toward the other leg.

This calf muscle pulls on the heel to bend your foot downward, such as when standing on tiptoe.

The soleus bends your foot downward during walking, running, or jumping.

The quadriceps femoris straightens your leg at the knee, and bends it at the hip.

The sartorius bends your leg at the hip and turns it outward.

This shin muscle lifts your foot upward and tilts it inward.

This muscle straightens your toes and helps you bend your foot upward.

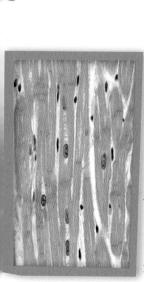

Heart muscle

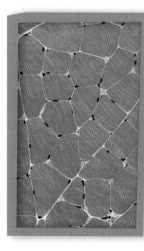

Skeletal muscle

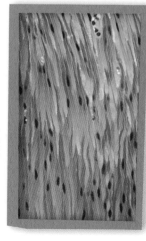

Smooth muscle

## Marvelous muscle

These microscopic views show the three types of muscle. Heart muscle has branching fibers (cells) that keep your heart beating. Skeletal muscle has long, thread-like fibers that pull your bones. Smooth muscle squeezes hollow organs, such as your stomach.

# Give it some muscle

The muscles that move your body are called skeletal muscles. They work by pulling the bones of your skeleton. But skeletal muscles can only pull, not push. So making a body part move in two directions needs different muscles that pull in opposite directions.

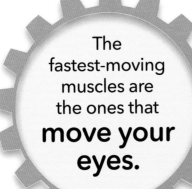

The fastest-moving muscles are the ones that **move your eyes.**

The hamstring muscles at the back of the thigh contract (shorten) and get fatter as they pull the leg backward and bend the knee. Try this with your biceps muscle—squeeze your upper arm with your left hand and then bend your right elbow. ..........

The knee joint bends when the lower leg is pulled by the hamstring muscles. The hamstrings also work to bend the upper leg backward at the hip. ..

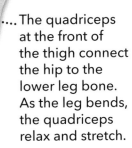

...The quadriceps at the front of the thigh connect the hip to the lower leg bone. As the leg bends, the quadriceps relax and stretch.

## Bending the leg

When you kick a ball, your leg first bends backward and then it moves forward. These movements in two directions need two sets of muscles, the quadriceps and the hamstrings, with opposite actions. To start the action, the hamstrings bend the leg.

## Straightening the leg

The job of straightening the leg belongs to the powerful quadriceps. By going against the action of the hamstrings, they straighten the leg at the knee. They also swing the leg forward by straightening the leg at the hip. Now your foot can hit the ball with its full force.

## Inside a muscle

This close-up view inside a skeletal muscle shows bundles of muscle fibers (red). Fibers are long cells that look like rods and run along the length of the muscle. When they receive a signal from the brain, muscle fibers get shorter. This makes the muscle pull on bones to make them move.

The free-moving joint between the top of the thigh bone and the hip bone allows a wide range of movement including backward and forward.

The hamstring muscles at the back of the thigh also connect the hip and lower leg bones. When the leg straightens, they relax and stretch.

The quadriceps contract to pull the thigh forward and straighten the knee. You can feel this fleshy muscle group, one of the body's strongest, in your thigh.

Control Center

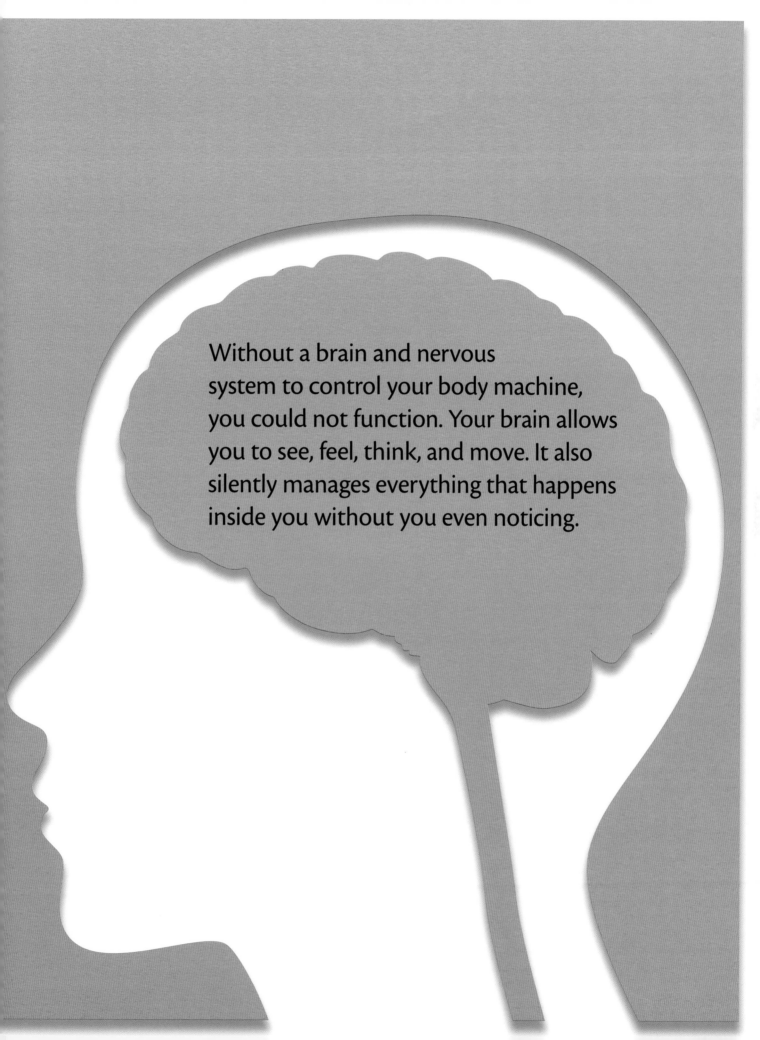

Without a brain and nervous system to control your body machine, you could not function. Your brain allows you to see, feel, think, and move. It also silently manages everything that happens inside you without you even noticing.

# Nerve network

Whether it's running or seeing, or thinking or breathing, almost everything your body machine does is controlled by your nervous system. It works really quickly because nerve cells carry messages that flash at high speed through the brain, spinal cord, and nerves.

## Wired up

The brain and the spinal cord are in control of your nervous system. They receive signals and send out instructions through a network of nerves. Each nerve contains bundles of long nerve cells. They carry signals to and from every part of your body.

The longest nerves in the human body are **more than 3 ft (1 m) long.**

The brain, the control center of the nervous system, sends and receives messages along nerves.

This is one of 31 nerves that branch out from each side of the spinal cord.

The spinal cord carries signals between the brain and the rest of the body.

The radial nerve connects to the skin and muscles of the arm.

There are twelve pairs of intercostal nerves that carry messages to the rib muscles, which allow you to breathe.

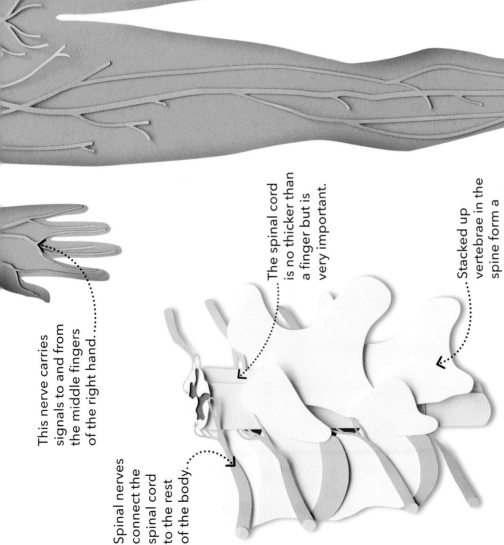

The sciatic nerve, the thickest and longest nerve in the body, sends messages to the leg, including the muscles that make you walk.

The peroneal nerve supplies the lower leg and carries the signals that tell the foot to bend.

This is one of the nerves that carries messages to and from the toes.

This nerve carries signals to and from the middle fingers of the right hand.

The spinal cord is no thicker than a finger but is very important.

Stacked up vertebrae in the spine form a tunnel around the spinal cord.

Spinal nerves connect the spinal cord to the rest of the body.

## Spinal cord

Starting from your brain, your spinal cord runs down your back. To protect it from damage, it is surrounded by the bones of the spine. It carries messages to and from your brain and body. It also controls quick reflexes, such as pulling your hand away from something hot or sharp.

# Wired up

Your nervous system includes your brain, spinal cord, and nerves. It is wired up with billions of long nerve cells called neurons. These special cells create and carry tiny electrical signals, called nerve impulses, which whizz around your body.

Incoming signals travel toward the ending of the nerve fiber.

The nucleus is the neuron's control center.

Nerve impulses move along the nerve fiber of the first neuron toward the second neuron.

The first neuron makes nerve impulses to send to a second neuron.

The ending of one neuron meets the dendrite of another neuron at a gap, called a synapse.

## Nerve impulses

Each neuron is in contact with lots of other neurons in your brain, creating a massive network for sending and receiving messages. Those messages take the form of nerve impulses that travel, in one direction, along one neuron before being picked up by another neuron. Where neurons meet, at gaps called synapses, chemicals carry signals across the gap.

Nerve fiber endings connect with other neurons at synapses.

Branching arms, called dendrites, receive signals from other neurons.

Signals are sent along the nerve fiber of the second neuron.

A protective cover insulates the nerve fiber, making nerve impulses travel much faster.

Nerve impulses flash along neurons at speeds over **275 mph (400 kph).**

# Living computer

A computer does all sorts of jobs for us. Your brain is like a living computer, remembering, processing information, and sending out instructions. But it is better and far faster than a computer. Nerve cells in the brain send millions of messages to each other every second.

Your brain contains billions of nerve cells that form a connecting network.

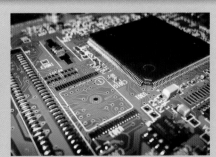

The black chip is a key part of a computer that processes information like your brain, but it is far less complicated.

# Headquarters

Locked securely inside your head is the soft organ that controls you. Your brain lets you move and feel, think and speak, remember and imagine. It also silently manages your heart rate, breathing, and many other essential activities.

## Inside the brain

This brain is sliced in half to show its three main parts—the cerebrum, cerebellum, and brain stem. The powerful cerebrum makes up the largest part of your brain and has left and right halves. The left brain controls the right side of the body, and the right brain controls the left. Here you can see the inside of the right half of the brain. Because its surface is wrinkled, it allows more thinking power to be squeezed inside the skull.

The human brain is the most **complex organ** in the living world.

This part, called the hypothalamus, controls many things, including sleep, body temperature, hunger, and thirst.

This gland is called the pituitary gland. It releases hormones, and is linked to the hypothalamus.

The brain stem manages basic activities such as breathing and heart rate.

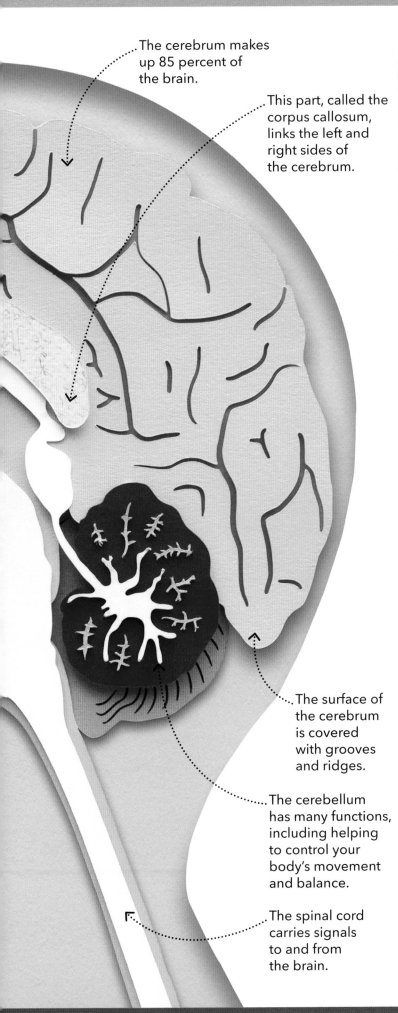

The cerebrum makes up 85 percent of the brain.

This part, called the corpus callosum, links the left and right sides of the cerebrum.

The surface of the cerebrum is covered with grooves and ridges.

The cerebellum has many functions, including helping to control your body's movement and balance.

The spinal cord carries signals to and from the brain.

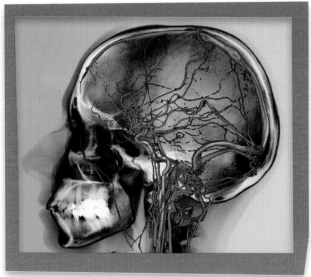

## Feed me

Here you can see the arteries (red) that carry food and oxygen to the brain, and the veins (blue) that remove its waste. Food and oxygen give the brain the energy it needs to work. If that supply is stopped, even for a few minutes, the brain may be damaged or even die.

## Brain protectors

Your brain is soft, like a mushroom, and it would be damaged if not protected from knocks and blows. Your skull does that by providing a hard case around your brain, like this hard baseball hat protects its wearer from injury. The brain is also protected by fluid which surrounds it and absorbs hard knocks.

# Mind map

The most important part of your brain is the cerebrum, in particular, its thin, wrinkly outer layer, called the cerebral cortex. Here, billions of nerve cells linked by trillions of connections make your body work and make you, you.

## Brain at work

This brain map shows how each area of the cerebral cortex has its own job. Some areas receive signals from the body. Others send instructions to the body. Some analyze and make sense of messages. Different areas of your cortex interact so you can understand, decide, think, move, feel, and remember. Parts of the cortex can grow large with constant use—so, for example, musicians often have a larger auditory (hearing) cortex.

The premotor cortex controls skillked movements, such as riding a bike.

The motor cortex tells your skeletal muscles to produce body movements.

This area, called the prefontal cortex, is involved with personality, and with thinking, learning, and understanding.

Broca's area controls speaking.

This area, called the auditory cortex, processes sounds.

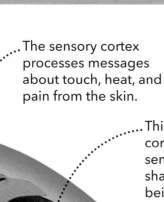

The sensory cortex processes messages about touch, heat, and pain from the skin.

This part of the cortex identifies skin sensations and the shape of objects being felt.

The visual cortex puts together messages to create images that you can see.

Wernicke's area figures out the meanings of words that are heard or seen.

The primary visual cortex receives signals from your eyes.

This area, called the auditory association cortex, analyzes signals from the hearing area to identify sounds.

The cerebellum sits below the cerebrum, and manages movement and balance.

The **125 trillion** connections between brain cells create a huge, super-fast communication network.

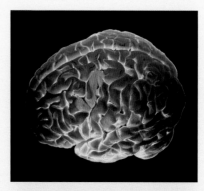

The active part of the cortex shown here includes Broca's area, which controls speech.

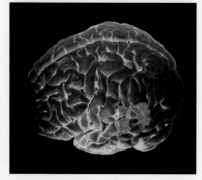

A fraction of a second after the brain's hearing areas detect sounds, another part figures out what is being said.

# Seeing the brain

These two brain scans show the active parts of a person's cerebral cortex lit up in red and green: first, when a person is speaking, and second, when understanding the words that were spoken.

# Sleep mode

Everybody needs sleep. During a lifetime, people spend one-third of each day asleep. Without sleep, your body machine would not survive. Sleep gives your body a chance to relax and recover, and gives your brain time to sort out the day's events.

## Fast asleep

When you sleep, your breathing and heart rate slow down. At first you go into a deep sleep, and it is difficult to wake up. Then you pass into dreaming sleep, when your brain is busier and you dream. These stages of sleep happen several times each night.

Your ears ignore everyday sounds but pick up sudden, strange noises.

Your eyelids close, and your eyes do not move much, except during dreaming sleep.

The fleshy flap at the back of your mouth may vibrate and cause snoring.

## Dream machine

Almost everyone dreams, but no one really knows why. Dreams often involve strange, mixed-up images of people and events that would not happen in real life. When you dream, your body's muscles, apart from your eye muscles, stop working. Because of this, you cannot act out your dream.

People often dream about being chased.

A feeling of falling through the air is common in dreams.

## How much sleep do you need?

The number of hours we spend asleep gets less as we get older. Babies spend more than half their day asleep. School-age children need between nine and eleven hours. Adults need up to nine hours, and they need less sleep as they age.

 Newborn babies 14–17 hours

 Children 9–11 hours

 Adults 7–9 hours

 Older people 7–8 hours

# Seeing

Most of what you know about the world comes to you through your sense of sight. Your eyes pick up light from objects. They pass this information to your brain, so you can see the world around you.

## How we see

Light rays enter your eye through a window called the cornea. The rays pass through a hole called the pupil and enter the lens. The lens changes shape to focus the light at the back of the eye, making an upside-down image. When signals from the eyes reach the brain, it creates an image that is the right way up.

....Object

....Light rays

The cornea bends light rays as they enter the eye....

Watery fluid, called the aqueous humor, fills the front part of the eye....

The pupil lets light into the eye...

The iris controls how much light comes into the eye...

The lens changes shape to focus light...

The sclera is a tough layer that protects the eyeball....

## Near and far

The lens in your eye changes shape to focus light from an object so that you can see it clearly. Tiny muscles in a ring around the lens squeeze, the lens gets fatter, and you can see objects close by. The muscles relax to flatten the lens, so that you can focus on objects farther away.

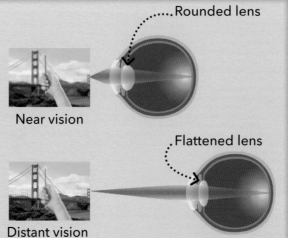

....Rounded lens

Near vision

.Flattened lens

Distant vision

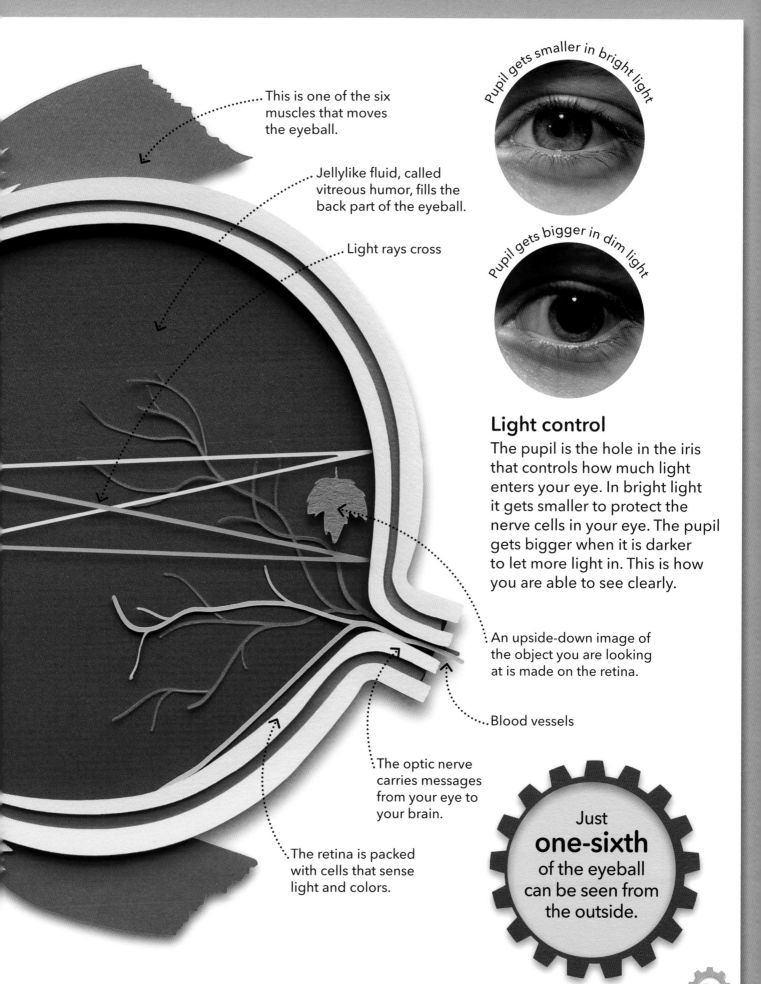

This is one of the six muscles that moves the eyeball.

Jellylike fluid, called vitreous humor, fills the back part of the eyeball.

Light rays cross

Pupil gets smaller in bright light

Pupil gets bigger in dim light

## Light control

The pupil is the hole in the iris that controls how much light enters your eye. In bright light it gets smaller to protect the nerve cells in your eye. The pupil gets bigger when it is darker to let more light in. This is how you are able to see clearly.

An upside-down image of the object you are looking at is made on the retina.

Blood vessels

The optic nerve carries messages from your eye to your brain.

The retina is packed with cells that sense light and colors.

Just **one-sixth** of the eyeball can be seen from the outside.

# Hearing

From the rustle of leaves to the roar of a jet plane, you can hear a wide range of sounds. Sounds are made when something vibrates and sends ripples through the air. Those ripples make vibrations in your ears that are turned into sounds by your brain.

Most parts of the ear are hidden inside the head.

This nerve carries signals about sounds from the cochlea to the hearing part of the brain.

These three tubes are filled with fluid, so may pick up movements of the head and help the body stay balanced.

These three linked bones are called ossicles. They carry sounds from the eardrum to the cochlea.

The cochlea is coiled like a snail's shell and detects sounds.

The eardrum vibrates when it is hit by sounds.

This tube connects the ear to your throat and nose. It lets in air, making your ears "pop" to clear away any blockage.

## Inside the ear

The only part of your ear that you can see is the outer flap. The rest is tucked inside your skull. Sounds from the outside world make vibrations that reach the coiled cochlea deep in the ear. Here vibrations are turned into nerve signals that go to the hearing area of your brain.

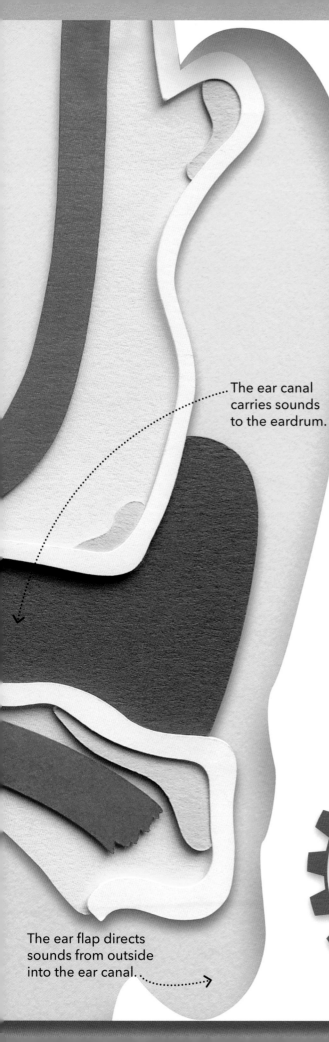

...The ear canal carries sounds to the eardrum.

The ear flap directs sounds from outside into the ear canal...

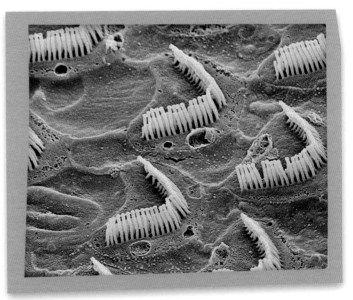

## Sound detectors

The cochlea contains tiny, V-shaped tufts of "hairs" (the pink strands above). They sit on top of special hair cells that detect sounds. Sound vibrations passing through the cochlea bend the "hairs." This makes the hair cells send signals to the brain, so you hear sounds.

## Balancing act

Your ears help you balance. Next to the cochlea are sensors that pick up the movement and position of your head. Your brain uses this information, together with signals from your eyes, muscles, and feet, to tell you how to move so you do not fall down.

The **smallest bone** is inside your ear and is the size of a **grain of rice.**

# Taste and smell

The smell of baking bread, the scent of flowers, and the taste of ice cream are all picked up by your senses of taste and smell. As well as working on their own, these two senses work together so that you can enjoy lots of different flavors.

## Mouth and nose

Special receptors on your tongue sense taste. Receptors that pick out smells are in a space behind your nose, called the nasal cavity. Your tongue senses five tastes: sweet, sour, bitter, salty, and a savory taste called umami. Smell receptors can pick up many different smells.

Your brain tells you what the tastes and smells are.

Smell receptors pick out smells in the air you breathe in.

This nerve carries signals from smell receptors to your brain.

Air breathed in through your nostrils carries smells into your nasal cavity.

Food and drink taken into the mouth contain tastes.

We can pick out **millions** of different smells, but only have five **different tastes.**

The surface of the tongue has taste receptors called taste buds.

These nerves carry signals from the taste detectors to your brain.

A row of big papillae sit at the back of the tongue.......

## Tasting tongue

Look in a mirror and you will see that your tongue is covered in tiny bumps. They are called papillae and there are three different types, as shown here. The big papillae and those that are mushroom-shaped have taste buds that detect the five tastes in food and drink.

Mushroom-shaped papillae are dotted all over the tongue.

Spiky papillae grip food while you are chewing.

## Bad tastes and smells

Your senses of smell and taste can tell you when something is wrong. A bitter or sour taste can sometimes mean that food is poisonous, although some poisons do not taste like anything. A smell of smoke may warn you about possible danger. Tasting or smelling something really disgusting makes your nose wrinkle and lips curl.

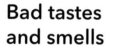

# How you feel

There are millions of tiny nerve cells, called touch receptors, in your skin. They detect changes in the texture, pressure, movements, and temperature of your surroundings. They send signals to your brain that allow you to sense the world around you.

## How sensitive?

This odd-looking figure is called a homunculus. It has been used for many years to show how parts of the body vary in their sensitivity. Some body parts, such as the lips and the tongue, are shown really big to reflect how they are particularly sensitive to touch.

Ears, as shown by their size, are sensitive to touch.

Lips are very sensitive, especially to touch and cold.

The tongue senses touch, pressure, heat, and cold, and also has taste detectors.

Touch receptors in the skin of the arm are well spaced out.

Hands are very sensitive to pressure and vibrations.

Fingertips are packed with more receptors, including pain receptors, than other skin areas.

The lower back has the body's least sensitive skin.

# Fingertips

can feel tiny bumps on a surface that are less than 0.03 in (1 mm) high.

## Brain connections

Signals from the skin are sent to the brain's sensory cortex. This picture shows the two halves of the brain's cerebrum and which parts of the brain link with which parts of the body. It shows that more sensitive body parts take up more space in the sensory cortex.

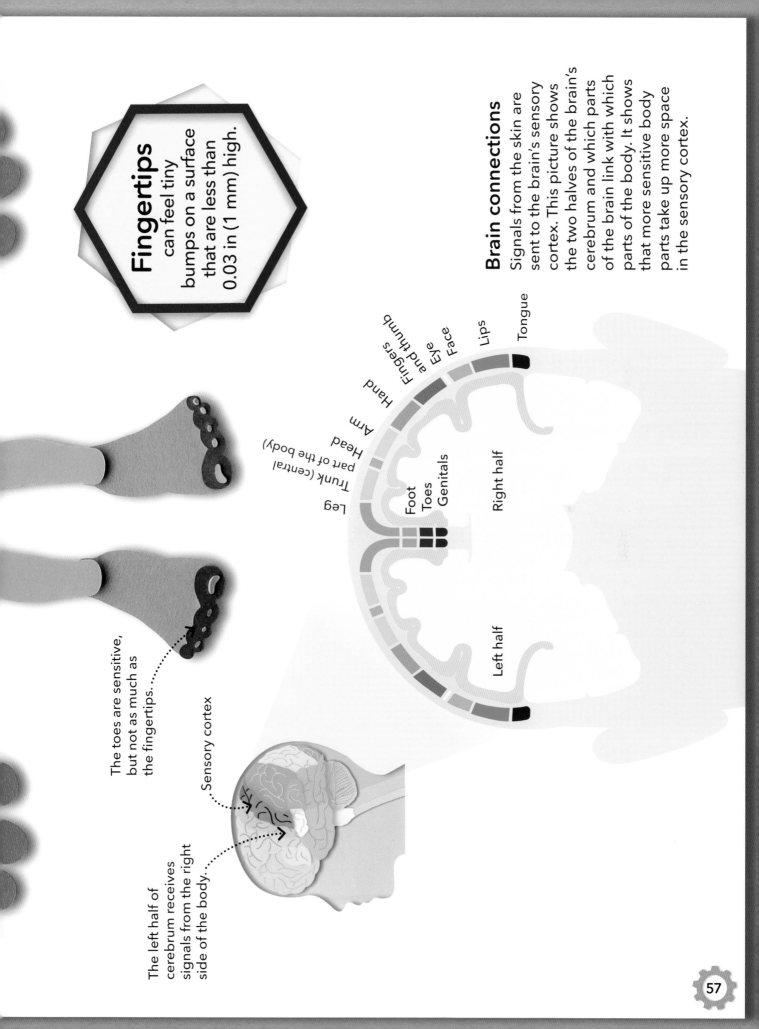

Tongue
Lips
Face
Eye
Fingers and thumb
Hand
Arm
Head
Trunk (central part of the body)
Leg
Foot
Toes
Genitals

Right half

Left half

The toes are sensitive, but not as much as the fingertips.

Sensory cortex

The left half of cerebrum receives signals from the right side of the body.

# Chemical messengers

The body machine has two control systems. As well as the nervous system, there are chemical messengers called hormones. Hormones mostly travel in the blood. They alter how specific cells and tissues work to influence growth, digest food, use energy, and many other processes.

## Hormone makers

In this picture you can see some of the glands that make hormones. Organs, including the stomach and kidneys, also release hormones. Together these glands and organs make up the endocrine system.

The thyroid gland releases a hormone that makes cells work faster, and helps control body weight and temperature.

The four parathyroid glands make a hormone that controls levels of calcium, a chemical needed for healthy bones.

The adrenal glands release several hormones including adrenaline, which gets the body ready for action.

The pancreas releases hormones that control the amount of glucose in your blood.

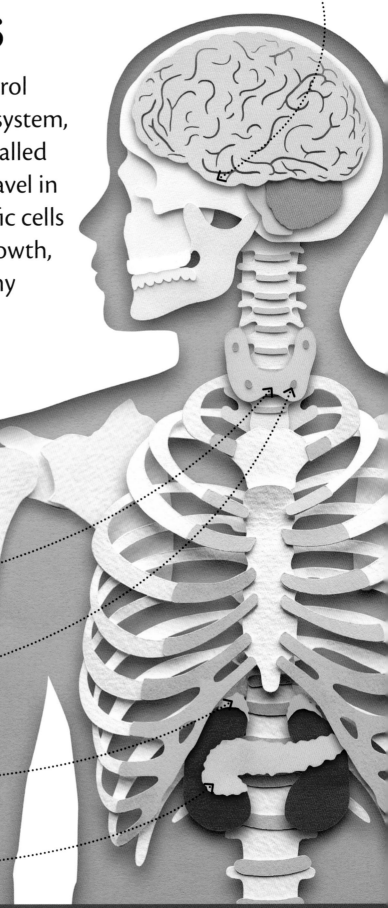

Tucked under the brain, the pituitary gland is very important. Many of its nine hormones circulate in the blood to control other glands like the thyroid.

## Cuddle chemical

Some hormones help with reproduction and birth. Oxytocin is one of the hormones released by the pituitary gland. It helps a woman to give birth to her baby by making her uterus squeeze, or contract. Oxytocin also helps create a close bond between a mother and her baby. For that reason it's called the "cuddle chemical."

When your **stomach is empty,** it releases a hormone that makes you feel hungry.

## Sugar control

Glucose is a sugar that supplies your cells with energy. Your pancreas makes several hormones, including insulin and glucagon. These two control the amount of glucose in the blood. In people with diabetes, the pancreas releases too little insulin. Diabetics need to take extra insulin to stop blood glucose levels becoming dangerously high.

This boy has diabetes. He is injecting himself with insulin using a special injector pen. ·······

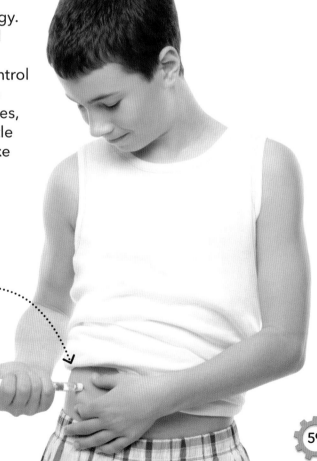

# Heart and Blood

The heart is at the core of your body machine, beating without a break all your life. Each beat pumps a red river of blood along a vast network of vessels. The blood supplies your body's cells with whatever they need to thrive and stay healthy.

# Blood flow

An amazing network of branching tubes, called blood vessels, carries blood all around your body. This blood supplies your body's cells with the food and oxygen they need to keep you alive. Blood is pumped along the blood vessels by your heart.

### Around the body

Here you can see some of the blood vessels that carry blood from your heart to all body parts and back again. Arteries (red) transport blood on its outward journey from the heart. Veins (blue) carry blood on its trip back.

This vein, called the jugular vein, carries blood from the head and brain toward the heart.

This artery, called the carotid artery, supplies the head and brain with blood.

The brachial artery carries blood that is rich in oxygen to the muscles and other parts of the arm.

The heart pumps blood along blood vessels.

The main artery leaving the heart is called the aorta. It is bigger than the width of an adult thumb.

This large vein, called the inferior vena cava, returns blood from the lower body to the heart.

There are **60,000 miles (100,000 km)** of blood vessels in your body—enough to stretch around the world twice!

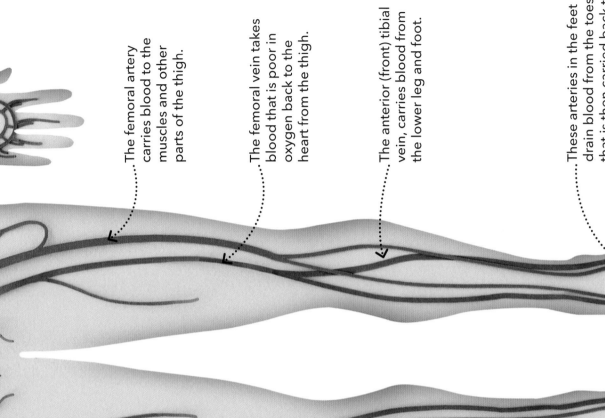

The femoral artery carries blood to the muscles and other parts of the thigh.

The femoral vein takes blood that is poor in oxygen back to the heart from the thigh.

The anterior (front) tibial vein, carries blood from the lower leg and foot.

These arteries in the feet drain blood from the toes that is then carried back to the heart.

**Artery**
Arteries have a thick, elastic wall that gets wider when the heart pumps blood through them.

**Vein**
Veins have a thinner wall than arteries and have valves to stop blood flowing backward.

**Capillary**
Capillaries are the smallest type of blood vessel. A capillary's wall is just one cell thick.

## Blood vessels

There are three different types of blood vessel. Arteries carry blood that is rich in oxygen away from your heart. Veins carry blood that is low in oxygen toward your heart. Tiny capillaries (too small to show in the main picture) connect arteries and veins, and give food and oxygen to cells.

# In the blood

Your blood vessels carry blood to and from all of your body's cells. Your heart beats constantly to pump this red, living liquid around your body thousands of times each day. Blood supplies your cells with everything they need to keep your body working.

## Blood cells

Your blood is made up of different types of cells. They float in a watery liquid called plasma. Red blood cells are the most common type of cell. They make blood red and carry oxygen. White blood cells fight germs. Small cell pieces, called platelets, help your blood to clot if you are wounded.

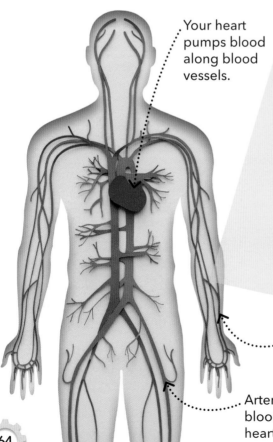

Your heart pumps blood along blood vessels.

Veins carry blood from the body to your heart.

Arteries carry blood from your heart to the body.

Red blood cells carry oxygen from your lungs to all parts of your body.

Plasma is the watery liquid in which blood cells and platelets float.

Platelets are small disk-shaped pieces of cell. They plug holes in damaged blood vessels by forming a clot.

White blood cells defend your body by destroying germs that cause disease.

A pinhead-sized drop of blood contains **2.5 million** red blood cells.

## Thicker blood

High up in the mountains, air contains less oxygen than at sea level. People who go mountain climbing struggle to breathe in enough oxygen at first. But gradually their bodies make extra red blood cells to get more oxygen from the air. These extra cells make their blood a bit thicker.

# Heartbeat

The same size as a fist, your heart is a powerful, muscular pump that pushes blood around your body. It beats without resting to supply your body with oxygen, nutrients, and other essentials, and to remove their waste.

## Receiving and sending

Your heart is two pumps in one, with separate right and left sides. The right side receives blood from the body and sends it to the lungs to pick up oxygen. The left side receives blood from your lungs and sends it to your body.

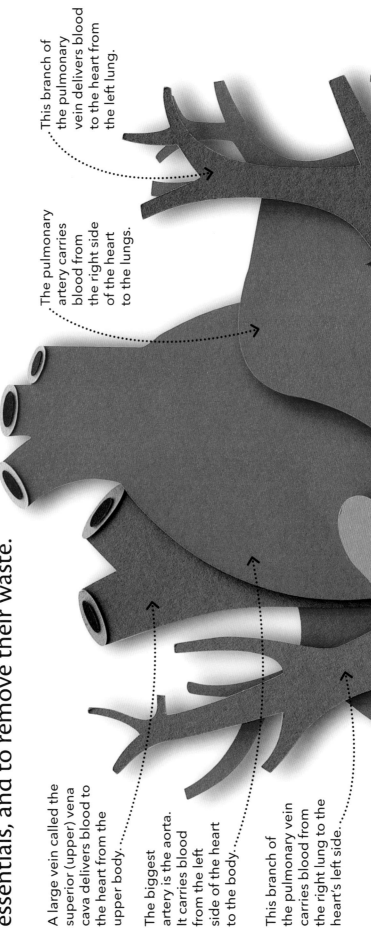

This branch of the pulmonary vein delivers blood to the heart from the left lung.

The pulmonary artery carries blood from the right side of the heart to the lungs.

A large vein called the superior (upper) vena cava delivers blood to the heart from the upper body.

The biggest artery is the aorta. It carries blood from the left side of the heart to the body.

This branch of the pulmonary vein carries blood from the right lung to the heart's left side.

This branch of the pulmonary artery carries blood to the left lung.

The heart's thick wall is made of muscle cells that tighten to make it beat without ever tiring.

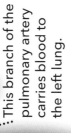

Your **heart beats** about **100,000 times each day** without a break.

A coronary artery supplies blood rich in oxygen to the heart's muscular wall.

A second large vein called the inferior (lower) vena cava carries blood to the heart from the lower body.

## Engine fuel

Just like a car's engine, your heart needs fuel and oxygen to keep it beating. These are carried by coronary arteries that wrap around the heart and send branches into its muscular wall. You can see them, in red, on this angiogram, a special type of X-ray.

# Feel the beat

When your heart beats, it lasts less than one second. During each beat, blood that is low in oxygen (blue) enters the right side of the heart and is pumped to the lungs. At the same time, blood that has lots of oxygen (red) enters the left side and is pumped to the body.

## The heart at work

Every time your heart beats, it pushes blood out and around your body. When the body needs more oxygen, such as during exercise, the heart beats faster. It can triple its speed. Here are the three stages of a heartbeat.

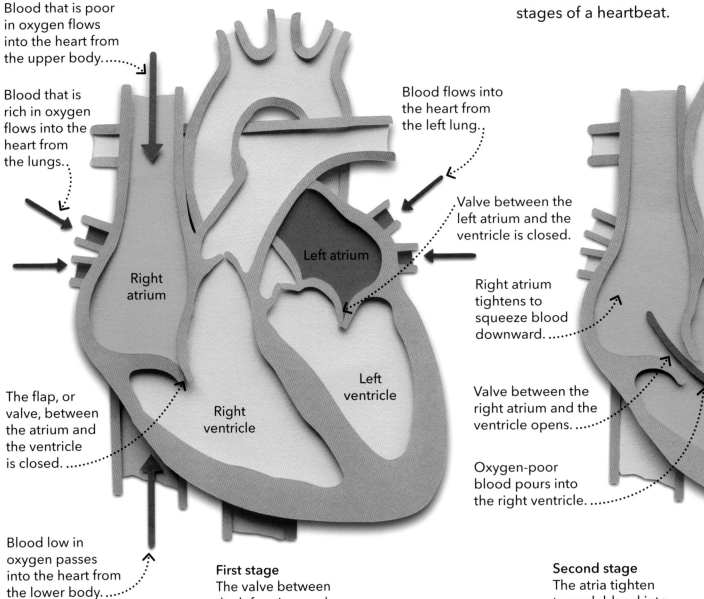

Blood that is poor in oxygen flows into the heart from the upper body.......

Blood that is rich in oxygen flows into the heart from the lungs..

Blood flows into the heart from the left lung..

..Valve between the left atrium and the ventricle is closed.

Left atrium

Right atrium

Right atrium tightens to squeeze blood downward. .......

The flap, or valve, between the atrium and the ventricle is closed. .......

Left ventricle

Right ventricle

Valve between the right atrium and the ventricle opens. .......

Oxygen-poor blood pours into the right ventricle. .......

Blood low in oxygen passes into the heart from the lower body.......

**First stage**
The valve between the left atrium and the ventricle is closed.

**Second stage**
The atria tighten to push blood into the lower chambers, called the ventricles.

# No way back

There are tiny flaps called valves inside your heart that make sure that blood flows in one direction during each heartbeat. When the heart tightens, the valves are forced open and blood flows through. When the heart relaxes, the valves close to stop blood flowing backward.

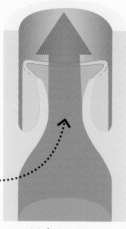

Blood gushes through the open valve when the heart pumps.

Valve open

Blood is trapped by the closed valve when the heart relaxes, and cannot flow back.

Valve closed

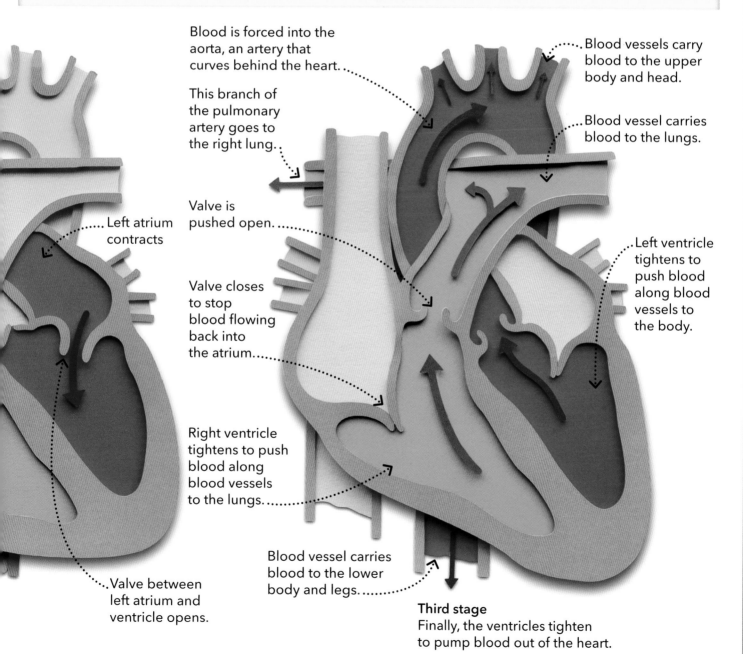

Blood is forced into the aorta, an artery that curves behind the heart.

This branch of the pulmonary artery goes to the right lung.

Blood vessels carry blood to the upper body and head.

Blood vessel carries blood to the lungs.

Left atrium contracts

Valve is pushed open.

Valve closes to stop blood flowing back into the atrium.

Left ventricle tightens to push blood along blood vessels to the body.

Right ventricle tightens to push blood along blood vessels to the lungs.

Valve between left atrium and ventricle opens.

Blood vessel carries blood to the lower body and legs.

**Third stage**
Finally, the ventricles tighten to pump blood out of the heart.

# Lungs and Breathing

You never take a break from breathing, even when you are asleep. The air you breathe into your lungs delivers the oxygen your cells need to release the energy that keeps them (and you) alive.

# Air supply

Your body's cells need a constant supply of oxygen. They use it to release the energy that keeps them working. As you breathe in oxygen, you also breathe out carbon dioxide, using your respiratory system.

## Nose to lungs

Your respiratory system consists of the airways and two lungs. Air rich in oxygen is breathed in through your nose, throat, and windpipe, called the trachea. It then passes inside the lungs along a network of airways. Air containing carbon dioxide is breathed out in the opposite direction.

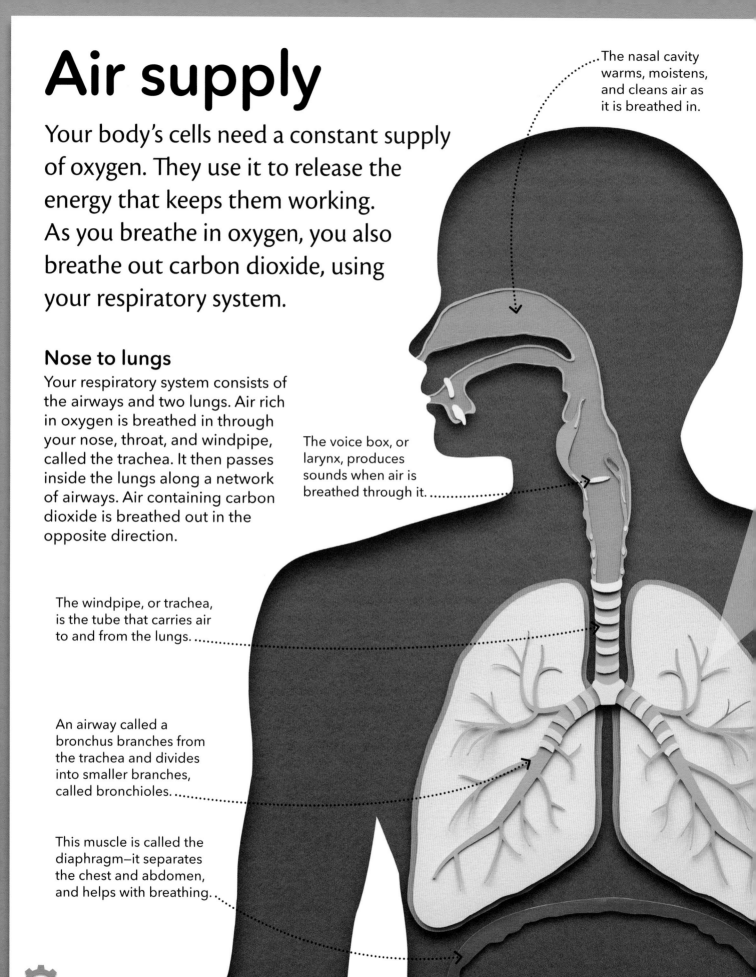

The nasal cavity warms, moistens, and cleans air as it is breathed in.

The voice box, or larynx, produces sounds when air is breathed through it.

The windpipe, or trachea, is the tube that carries air to and from the lungs.

An airway called a bronchus branches from the trachea and divides into smaller branches, called bronchioles.

This muscle is called the diaphragm—it separates the chest and abdomen, and helps with breathing.

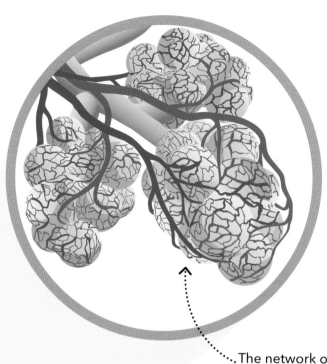

## Air bags

Each of your lung's 30,000 bronchioles ends in bunches of tiny air bags. These are where oxygen enters your blood and carbon dioxide comes out. Together, the air bags in both lungs provide a massive surface 35 times that of your skin, through which oxygen is quickly swapped for carbon dioxide.

The network of blood capillaries surrounding air bags delivers oxygen-poor blood (blue) and carries away oxygen-rich blood (red).

More than **2,500** of the lung's **tiny air bags** could fit onto your fingernail.

## Oxygen supply

You breathe in oxygen and breathe out carbon dioxide. So, what stops the planet's oxygen supply from running out? The answer is plants. During the day plants make their own food using sunlight. This process uses carbon dioxide and releases oxygen into the air.

Carbon dioxide

Oxygen

# Take a breath

Day and night, without a break, you breathe air into your lungs. Air contains oxygen, which your body needs. You breathe out stale air, containing waste carbon dioxide. Breathing makes sure that your body's cells have a non-stop supply of oxygen, and are not affected by carbon dioxide.

### In and out

Your lungs cannot move on their own to make you breathe. A curved muscle, called the diaphragm, helps with this. It works together with muscles between your ribs to get you breathing in and out.

Air that you breathe in through your nose and mouth has more oxygen and less carbon dioxide than air you breathe out.

Your lungs expand and suck in air from outside your body.

Your ribs move up and out to make your chest and lungs bigger.

The diaphragm tightens, flattens, and stretches your lungs downward.

**BREATHING IN**

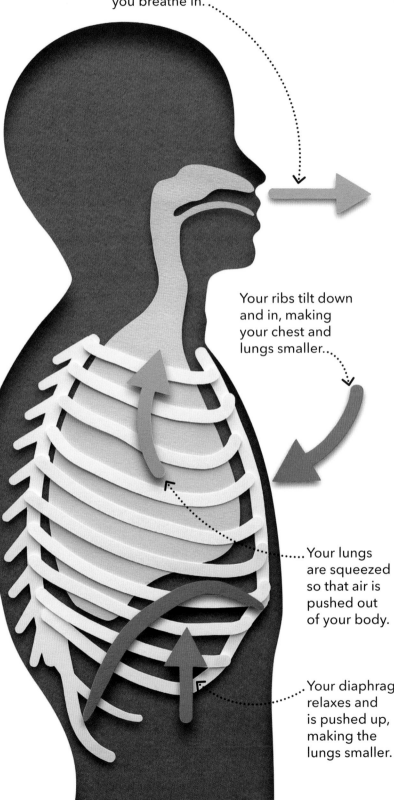

Air you breathe out contains less oxygen and more carbon dioxide than air you breathe in.

Your ribs tilt down and in, making your chest and lungs smaller...

Your lungs are squeezed so that air is pushed out of your body.

Your diaphragm relaxes and is pushed up, making the lungs smaller.

## Hold it

Unlike fish, humans cannot breathe under water. But some of us can stay under water for a minute or so by holding our breath. Some people, called free divers, can hold their breath for much longer and can dive to great depths of more than 700 ft (200 m).

**You breathe in and out** around **20,000** times each day.

**BREATHING OUT**

# Making noise

Only humans can communicate using speech. The sounds of speech are made by forcing bursts of air between folds in your throat known as vocal cords. These sounds are then shaped into words by the mouth.

## Making sounds

Your vocal cords stretch across your voice box in your throat. When they are pulled together, air forced between them makes them vibrate and produce sounds. These sounds are amplified by the voice box and the spaces, or cavities, in your throat and nose.

Muscles pull the voice box to tighten and close the vocal cords.

Vocal cords are pulled close together so that air from the lungs passes through a small gap.

## Breathing

When muscles in the wall of the voice box relax, the vocal cords open and separate. This allows air to move freely to and from the lungs along the windpipe.

The windpipe carries air to and from the lungs.

Vocal cords are relaxed and fully open during normal breathing.

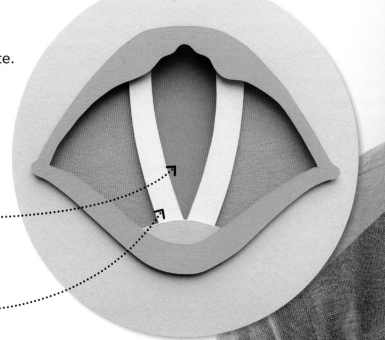

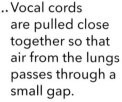

The human voice can range from a **whisper** to a shout as **loud** as a chainsaw.

Your tongue can touch your teeth, roof of your mouth, or pull backward.

Your lips can be pressed together, rounded, or pushed against the teeth.

## Shaping speech

The sounds made by your vocal cords are shaped into letters and words by your tongue, lips, and teeth. Under orders from your brain, they control the movement of air out of your mouth to create a full range of sounds.

## Snoring

Some people snore when they are asleep. Muscles relax, making the nasal passages and throat narrower. This slows down the movement of air to and from the lungs. As a result, parts of the nose, mouth, and throat vibrate, causing the person to snore.

# Out of control

Sneezing, yawning, and hiccups are some of the breathing movements that you cannot easily control. They are automatic reflex actions. Some of these actions help keep you healthy. Others, such as yawning, have no clear purpose, but may help you get more oxygen in your body to wake you up.

**Sneezes blast air out of the nose** at speeds of up to 100 mph (160 kph).

## Sneezing

A sneeze sends a noisy blast of air through your nose. It clears out itchy dust or germs. Sneezing happens when, after a sudden intake of breath, air is forced out of your lungs and upward through your nose. Coughing clears your throat in a similar way.

## Yawning

We all yawn, but we do not know why. It might be because we are tired or bored, or we might need to get extra air into our bodies. What we do know is that if you yawn, people around you will often yawn, too!

# Hiccups

The pictures below show what happens when you have hiccups. A muscle called the diaphragm tightens and air is sucked into your lungs. Your vocal cords slap together making a "hic." You might get hiccups if you eat too quickly.

Air is sucked in very quickly through your mouth.

Your two vocal cords snap shut, making the "hic" sound.

Your diaphragm suddenly tightens, flattens, and pulls air into the lungs.

Your vocal cords at the top of your windpipe open again.

Air is breathed out normally through your mouth and nose.

Your diaphragm relaxes, moving upward to push air out of your lungs.

# Under Attack

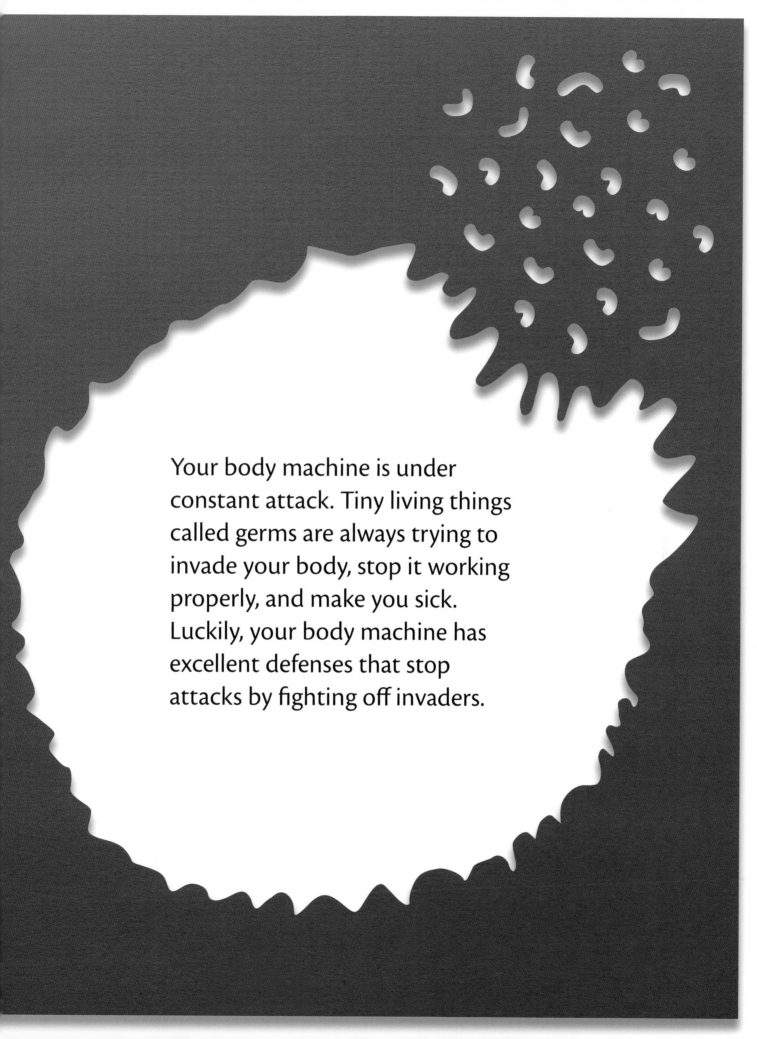

Your body machine is under constant attack. Tiny living things called germs are always trying to invade your body, stop it working properly, and make you sick. Luckily, your body machine has excellent defenses that stop attacks by fighting off invaders.

# Body defenses

Your body has clever ways of keeping you healthy. Your skin, for example, forms a barrier to stop germs getting inside you. Any germs that do get inside are tracked down and destroyed by white blood cells. Many of these cells live in your blood stream and lymphatic system.

## Lymphatic system

The tubes that make up your lymphatic system are called lymph vessels. They drain fluid, called lymph, from all parts of your body. As it travels, the lymph passes through tiny swellings in the lymph vessels, called lymph nodes. White blood cells inside the nodes pick out and destroy foreign bacteria.

Tonsils at the back of your mouth destroy bacteria in food, your saliva, and in your bloodstream.

Lymph empties into a vein here and flows into your blood.

The thymus gland trains white blood cells to become germ killers. It works particularly hard when you are growing.

Your spleen is an organ that contains germ-killing white blood cells. It also makes red and white blood cells.

A lymph node is a small swelling on a lymph vessel that filters lymph.

Lymph vessels are tubes that drain lymph from all parts of the body.

Bone marrow is inside bone. It makes red blood cells and also the white blood cells that kill germs.

Sweat spreading over the skin's surface helps to kill harmful germs.

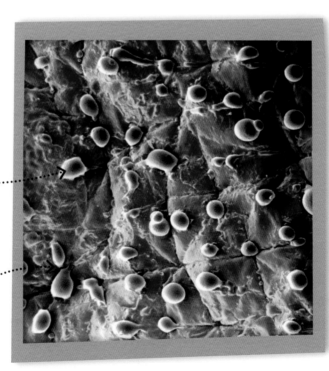

Sweat glands deep in your skin make sweat and release it onto the skin's surface.

## Skin and sweat

As well as stopping germs getting inside you, your skin also makes sweat, which contains germ-killing chemicals. If your skin is cut, these chemicals will quickly attack and kill any invading germs.

# Germs and disease

All around us there are millions and millions of tiny living things, too small to be seen. Most are harmless. Some, called germs, can cause disease. They get inside your body, multiply, and stop it working normally.

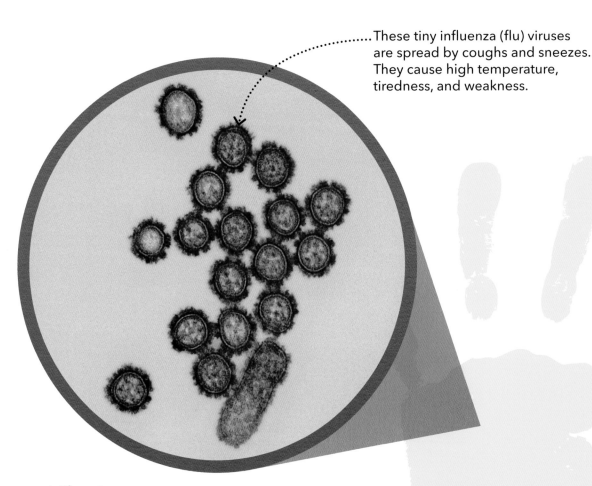

These tiny influenza (flu) viruses are spread by coughs and sneezes. They cause high temperature, tiredness, and weakness.

## Vile viruses

Viruses are the tiniest of all germs. They cause colds and flu as well as more serious diseases, such as measles and mumps. Viruses invade cells inside the body. They turn the cells into factories that produce even more viruses. Then the body's defense forces fight back and destroy them.

Dirty hands spread bacteria and viruses, such as when one person with a cold virus touches another person, and so spreads the virus.

## Biting bugs

Some diseases are spread by biting insects. This female mosquito is piercing a person's skin to feed on blood. Germs from her body are injected into the blood. Mosquitoes pass on several diseases including malaria, which can cause death if not treated quickly.

About **150** different types of bacteria **live on your hands.**

## Bad bacteria

Bacteria are bigger than viruses, but smaller than your body's cells. Many bacteria are harmless or even helpful. But if bad bacteria invade your body they release poisons called toxins. These can cause illnesses such as food poisoning or sore throats.

Salmonella bacteria cause food poisoning and get into the body when someone eats infected food such as infected eggs or chicken.

# Battle plan

Your body has a secret army that works unseen to protect it from germs that cause disease. Billions of white blood cells patrol the body, ready to do battle with invading germs. Germs include tiny, one-celled creatures called bacteria.

## Germ eaters

Many white blood cells are germ eaters. They travel around your body following germs. Here a germ eater, called a macrophage, prepares to grab and eat two bacteria before they can split and multiply to make an invading army.

Captured bacteria are soaked in powerful chemicals that kill them..

The bacteria are engulfed by the macrophage and trapped in a bag called a vesicle. They are then soaked in germ-killing liquid and destroyed.

The bacteria that cause disease are much smaller than a macrophage. They can divide very rapidly.

The macrophage checks the bacteria are "foreign" before surrounding them and pulling them inside it.

Macrophages are the largest white blood cells. Here a hungry macrophage makes contact with bacteria that have invaded the body. It changes shape so it can surround its enemies.

Bits and pieces left behind after the bacteria have been eaten are released from the macrophage.

Once the bacteria have been eaten, the macrophage throws out any unwanted waste. It then continues to search for more germs.

A macrophage **can eat about 200 bacteria** before it dies.

# Secret army

Several different types of white blood cells make up the secret army that defends your body day and night. You can see three of those types here. Both monocytes and neutrophils hunt and eat germs. Lymphocytes produce substances, which cause you to be immune to many infections.

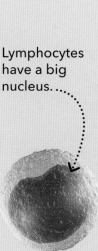

Lymphocytes have a big nucleus.

Monocytes become macrophages (germ eaters) when they leave your blood.

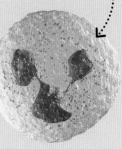

Neutrophils are the most common type of germ eater and help to control inflammation.

# Allergies

Your immune system defends you by destroying germs and harmful substances that are "foreign" to your body. But in some people, the system can attack foreign things too vigorously. The reaction, called an allergy, can make you sick.

Each of these is a tiny pollen grain magnified many times.

## Hay fever

One of the most common allergies is hay fever. It is set off by breathing in tiny pollen grains from plants. If a sensitive person's immune system attacks pollen grains, the lining of the nose and throat gets irritated. This causes sneezing, a runny nose, and itchy eyes.

## Asthma

This affects the lungs, and can be caused by an allergy to pollen, dust, or skin flakes. Asthma makes the airways inside the lungs narrow so that breathing becomes difficult. It can be treated using an inhaler, which helps widen the airways.

A boy with asthma uses an inhaler to get medicine into his lungs to help make breathing easier.

Pollen grains from the plant ragweed are a common cause of hay fever.

**Pollen grains** can travel up to **12.5 miles (20 km).**

Shellfish

Wheat

Eggs

## Food allergies

Allergies can be triggered by eating certain foods, such as the ones shown here. The effects may appear in minutes, or they might take hours. People can sometimes feel sick. More seriously, people can suffer swelling and breathing problems that may even need treatment by a doctor.

Milk

Peanuts

Cheese

# Fueling the Machine

When you eat and drink, you give your body machine the fuel it needs to stay alive and keep going. Inside your digestive system, food is broken down. This releases key nutrients that give your cells energy and allow them to build and replace themselves.

# Filling up

Several times each day you feel hungry, so you eat some food. That food gives you energy, helps you grow, and repairs your body machine. But first the food you eat has to be broken down into tiny pieces. That is the job of your digestive system.

## Digestive system

Your digestive system is a long tube that runs from your mouth, where food goes in, to the opening in your bottom (anus), where waste comes out. In between, food is broken down, or digested, by being chopped, crushed, and mixed with saliva, which contains chemicals called enzymes. Digestion releases simple substances, called nutrients, that your body can use.

Your throat carries food from the back of your mouth into a long tube called the esophagus.

As food enters your mouth, your lips close and your teeth cut and crush it into small pieces, preparing it for digestion.

Your tongue pushes a ball of chewed food into your throat.

The esophagus, carries food from your throat down to your stomach.

During an average lifetime, a person eats and digests at least **22 tons (20 metric tons)** of food.

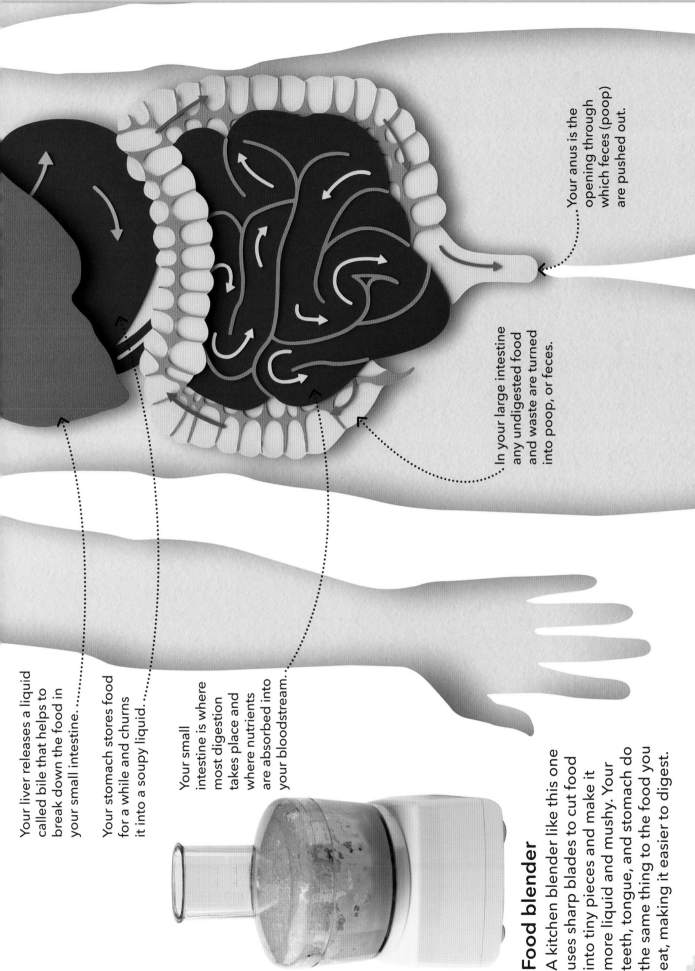

Your anus is the opening through which feces (poop) are pushed out.

In your large intestine any undigested food and waste are turned into poop, or feces.

Your liver releases a liquid called bile that helps to break down the food in your small intestine.

Your stomach stores food for a while and churns it into a soupy liquid.

Your small intestine is where most digestion takes place and where nutrients are absorbed into your bloodstream.

## Food blender

A kitchen blender like this one uses sharp blades to cut food into tiny pieces and make it more liquid and mushy. Your teeth, tongue, and stomach do the same thing to the food you eat, making it easier to digest.

# Open wide

Some animals, such as snakes, swallow their food whole. Humans cannot do that. Instead, inside your mouth, food is cut into small chunks, then ground up, mixed with saliva (spit), and swallowed.

## Chew and swallow

When you eat, your teeth slice and chew food into small pieces. The tongue moves food between your teeth and mixes it with slimy saliva. The ball of chewed food is pushed into your throat, swallowed, and travels to your stomach.

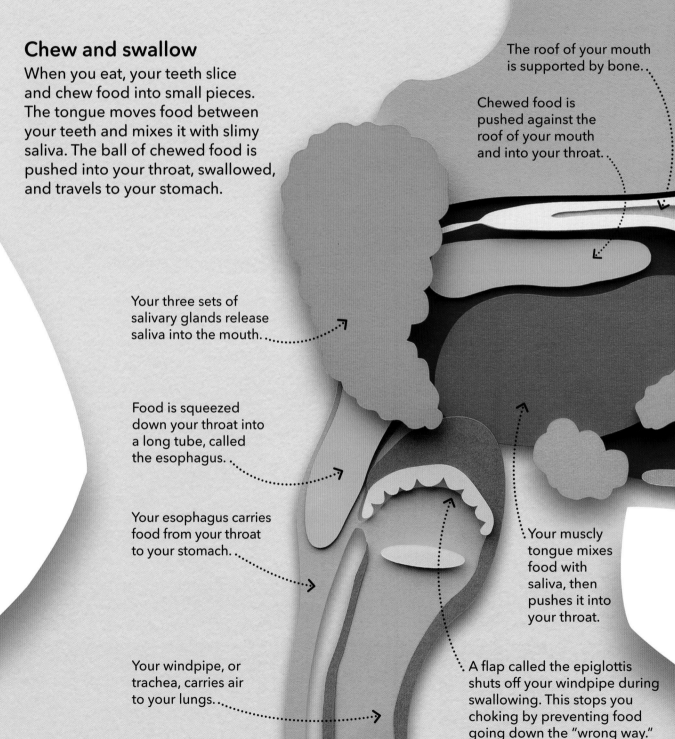

The roof of your mouth is supported by bone.

Chewed food is pushed against the roof of your mouth and into your throat.

Your three sets of salivary glands release saliva into the mouth.

Food is squeezed down your throat into a long tube, called the esophagus.

Your esophagus carries food from your throat to your stomach.

Your muscly tongue mixes food with saliva, then pushes it into your throat.

Your windpipe, or trachea, carries air to your lungs.

A flap called the epiglottis shuts off your windpipe during swallowing. This stops you choking by preventing food going down the "wrong way."

## Bite and crunch

This view inside a grown-up's mouth shows a full set of 32 teeth. It includes four different types of teeth, each with their own job to do. In each jaw there are four incisors, two canines, four premolars, and six molars. Younger children have 20 "baby" or "milk" teeth that are gradually replaced by adult teeth.

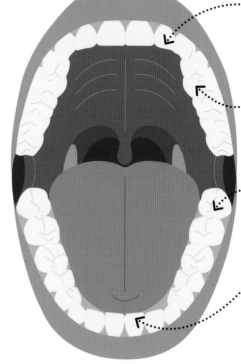

Canines are pointed teeth that grip and pierce food.

Premolars have two raised edges that help to crush food.

Molars are wide with a lumpy surface that grinds and crushes food.

Incisors are like knives that slice food into small chunks.

Your lips help to pull food into your mouth when you eat.

Your teeth are firmly anchored in your jawbones.

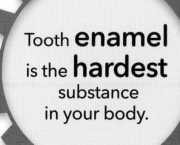

Tooth **enamel** is the **hardest** substance in your body.

## Cleaning your teeth

It is really important to brush your teeth to keep them healthy. Brushing removes old food, including sugar. If food is not removed, bacteria feed on the food that remains. Bacteria release acids that eat into the hard, white enamel covering your teeth, and cause tooth decay.

# In the stomach

Your stomach is a J-shaped bag that is tucked under your ribs. It has two important jobs to do. First it receives food you have just eaten and churns it up into a liquid. It then squirts this liquid into the small intestine.

## Mix and mash

The wall of your stomach is very stretchy and muscly. It gets bigger as it fills with food. The walls of your stomach squeeze the food and mix it with an acid juice, called gastric juice. A thick, soup-like liquid is formed. Muscles then propel it into the intestine when it is ready to leave.

...Food travels down a long tube, called the esophagus, and enters your stomach.

...The liquid will enter your small intestine, which finishes digesting it.

...A soupy liquid is made as your stomach squeezes and churns food.

...Three muscle layers wrap around your stomach.

# Store, churn, and release

Once you have eaten a meal, your stomach stores swallowed food for about three hours.

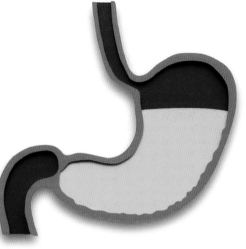

**Filling**
During a meal the stomach starts to fill up with chewed food and gets bigger as its wall stretches. Sometimes the gases caused by digestion go back up the esophagus and cause you to burp or even belch.

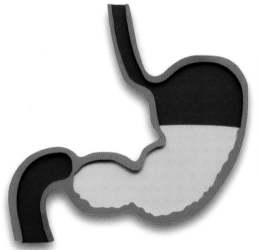

**Digestion**
One to two hours after eating, food is part-digested by gastric juice and churned into creamy liquid.

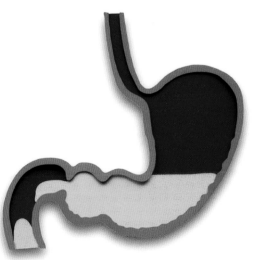

**Emptying**
Three to four hours after eating, the end of the stomach opens and enters the small intestine.

An adult's **stomach** can stretch to **20 times** its normal size after a meal.

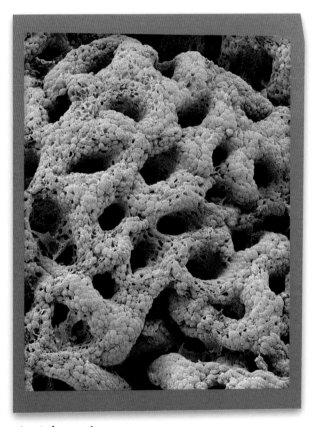

## Acid makers

This close-up view of the stomach's lining shows lots of holes. These are the entrances to the glands that release gastric juice into the stomach during digestion. Gastric juice contains strong acid that kills germs, and enzymes that digest proteins in food.

# Tangled tubes

Coiled below your stomach are tubes called the intestines. The long and narrow small intestine finishes off digestion, soaking up everything your body needs. It is particularly important for digesting vegetables. The large intestine gets rid of any leftover waste.

## Long journey

Food takes many hours to travel through your intestines. As it journeys through your small intestine it is broken down into simple nutrients that your body can use. The nutrients pass into your blood. Any leftover waste is turned into feces (poop) by your large intestine and pushed out of your body.

An adult's **small intestine** is an incredible **20 ft (6 m)** long.

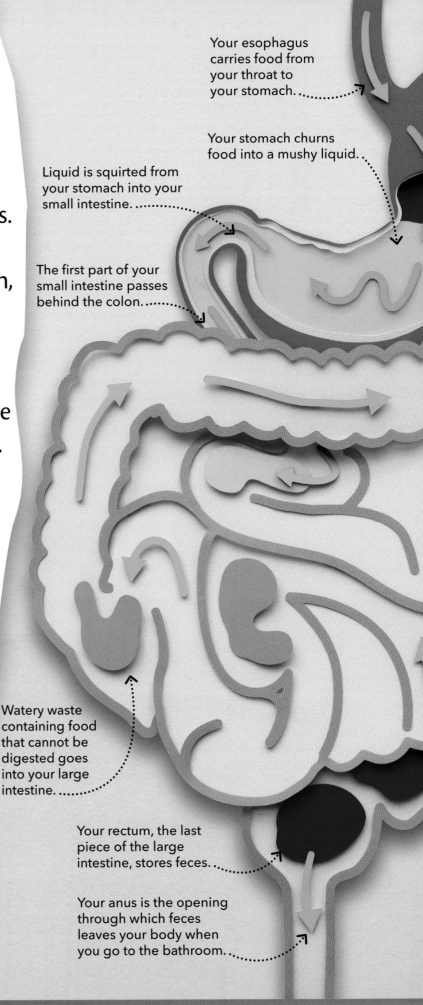

Your esophagus carries food from your throat to your stomach.

Your stomach churns food into a mushy liquid.

Liquid is squirted from your stomach into your small intestine.

The first part of your small intestine passes behind the colon.

Watery waste containing food that cannot be digested goes into your large intestine.

Your rectum, the last piece of the large intestine, stores feces.

Your anus is the opening through which feces leaves your body when you go to the bathroom.

## Keep squeezing

Food is squeezed along your digestive system by a process called peristalsis. Muscles tighten and relax in waves to push food through your intestines. It is a little like using your fingers to squeeze toothpaste out of a tube.

Muscles squeeze behind the ball of food.

Muscles relax so the intestine bulges out, allowing food to move onward.

The colon, the longest part of the large intestine, loops around the small intestine.

Water is soaked up from waste as it passes along the colon to form brown feces.

Food moves down the intestine as waves of squeezing and relaxing push it along.

Food is digested in your small intestine, where nutrients that your body needs enter the blood.

## Villi lining

Magnified many times, these are villi, the tiny "fingers" that line your small intestine. These villi increase the surface area of the inside of your intestine, and this helps nutrients to be absorbed quickly. From here, nutrients pass into your blood and travel on to your body's cells.

# Cleaning station

The liver is a very important chemical factory. Millions of cells inside this big organ keep your body machine working properly. The liver has around 500 different jobs. Among the most important are processing and "cleaning" the blood.

## Inside your liver

This view inside your liver shows that it has two blood supplies. An artery delivers oxygen, while a vein brings in nutrients from the food you have just eaten. Your liver sorts the nutrients, storing some and sending the rest to your body's cells. It also destroys poisons and releases heat to keep you warm.

Branches of this vein carry blood rich in food to cells in your liver.

The gallbladder is a bag that stores bile, a liquid made in the liver that helps you digest fatty food.

The bile duct carries bile from your gallbladder to your small intestine.

The largest artery in the body is called the aorta. It carries blood from your heart to the rest of your body.

This vein carries "cleaned" blood out of your liver.

**Your liver** is the **biggest organ** inside your body.

This artery delivers blood full of oxygen to your liver.

This vein carries blood rich in food from the digestive system to the liver.

## Sugar control

One of your liver's jobs is to store glucose, the sugar that gives your cells energy. If there is too little glucose in your blood, your liver releases more. If there is too much glucose, after you have a sugary drink for example, your liver stores the extra glucose.

# The right fuel

To get the right fuel for your body, you should eat a good variety of different foods, so you stay healthy. Food supplies your body with the things it needs to give it energy, make it grow, and keep it alive.

## Balanced diet

This guide shows you the general proportions of different foods that will give you a good balanced diet and keep you healthy. Water is important, too. It is found not only in drinks but also in most foods, especially fruit and vegetables.

## Drinking water

Water makes up more than 50 percent of your body, and it is an essential part of your diet. Without water, your cells could not work, so your body machine would break down.

Vegetables are packed with vitamins and minerals to keep you healthy.

Fruit contains lots of vitamins. It also provides sugars for energy, and fiber for a healthy digestive system.

Bread, pasta, and rice contain carbohydrates, which give you energy.

Olives are the source of olive oil that, like other healthy oils and fats, helps to build cells.

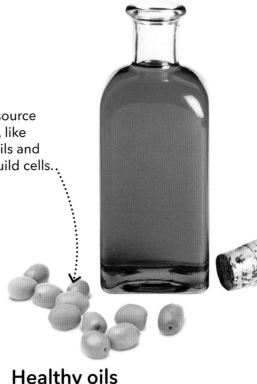

## Healthy oils

Eating small amounts of oils found in plants, such as olives, and oily fish, such as salmon, is really important for good health. These oils contain fatty acids, which help keep the brain and other organs working properly.

Fish, chicken, beans, lentils, nuts, and meat contain protein that is needed for growth and repair.

Milk and other dairy foods provide calcium, needed for healthy bones and teeth.

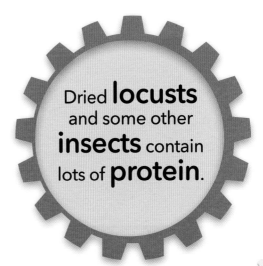

Dried **locusts** and some other **insects** contain lots of **protein**.

Waterworks

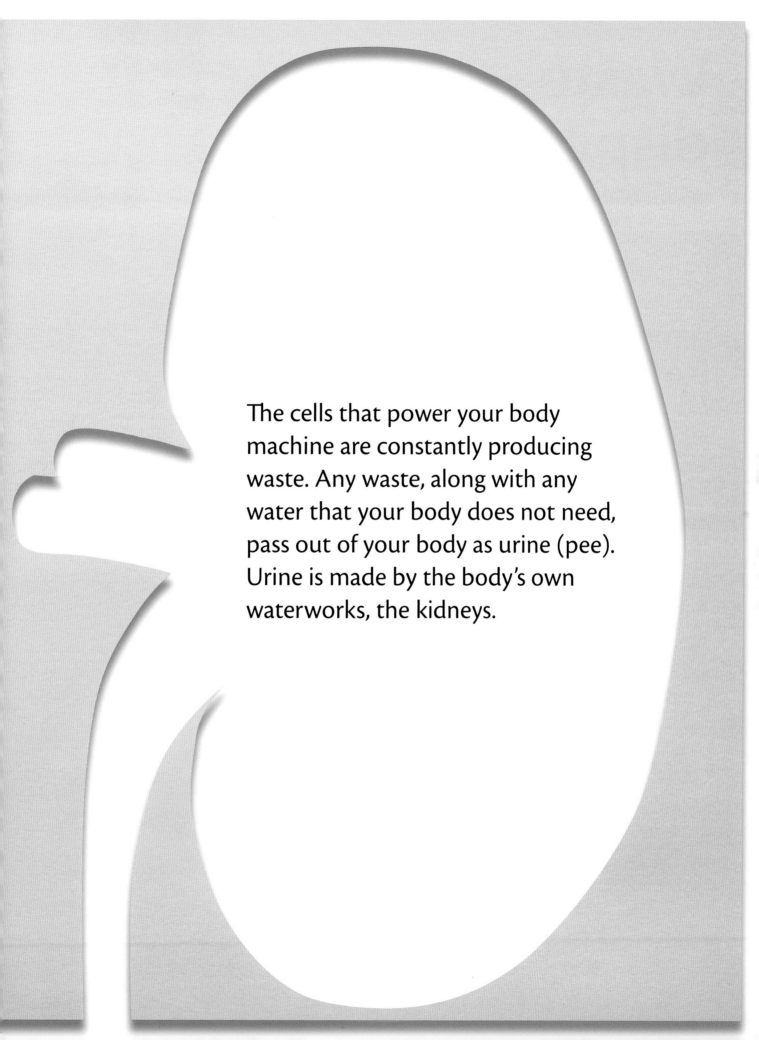

The cells that power your body machine are constantly producing waste. Any waste, along with any water that your body does not need, pass out of your body as urine (pee). Urine is made by the body's own waterworks, the kidneys.

# Waste disposal

Waste from your body's cells needs to be removed from your blood. This is the job of your urinary system. As your blood passes through your two kidneys, it is cleaned. Any waste and unwanted water eave your body as urine.

Your right kidney, and the left kidney opposite it, filter blood to make urine (pee). ......

A tube called the ureter carries freshly made urine from a kidney to your bladder. ..

Your bladder is a stretchy bag that stores urine until you are ready to go to the bathroom...

Another tube, called the urethra, carries urine out of your body when you pee. ...

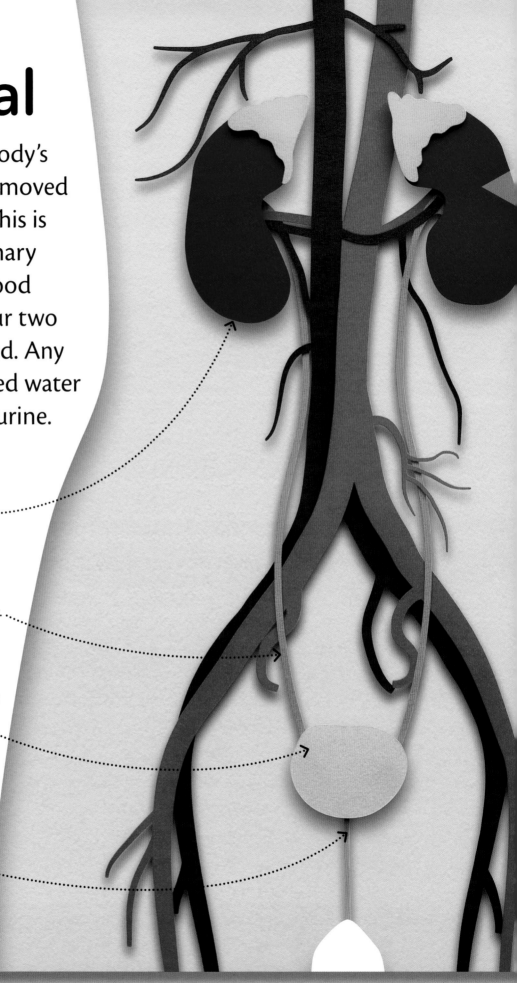

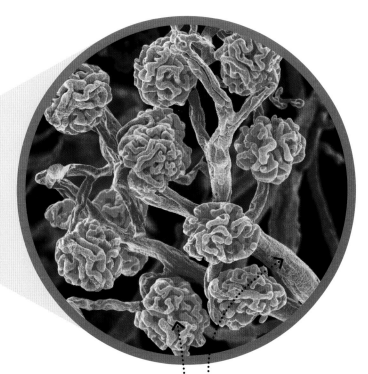

## Urinary system

Your urinary system is made up of two kidneys, two ureters, the bladder, and the urethra. While blood flows through the kidneys, fluid passes out of it. As that fluid flows through millions of special filters, substances that the body needs, such as sugars, return to the blood. Any remaining water and wastes leave the kidney as urine.

Fluid leaves the blood as it passes through these bundles of capillaries.

This is one of the branches of the artery that carries blood to be cleaned into the kidney.

**Each day**
the kidneys filter 48 gallons (180 liters) of fluid from the blood.

## Dialysis machine

Sometimes a person's kidneys stop working properly. If this happens they can be connected to a machine that cleans their blood for them. This is called a dialysis machine. As blood flows from the person, through the machine and back again, it is filtered and cleaned. Without dialysis that person would become very sick.

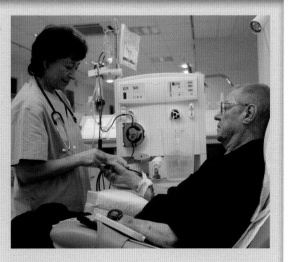

# Full and empty

Your two kidneys produce a steady trickle of urine (pee) throughout the day. Without your bladder, urine would dribble out of the body, making life very uncomfortable. Your bladder stores urine, then releases it when you go to the bathroom.

## Store and release

Your bladder stretches as it fills up with urine. A tube at the bottom of the bladder, called the urethra, carries urine out of the body. Normally the urethra is closed by muscles, but when the bladder is full, those muscles relax and urine flows out.

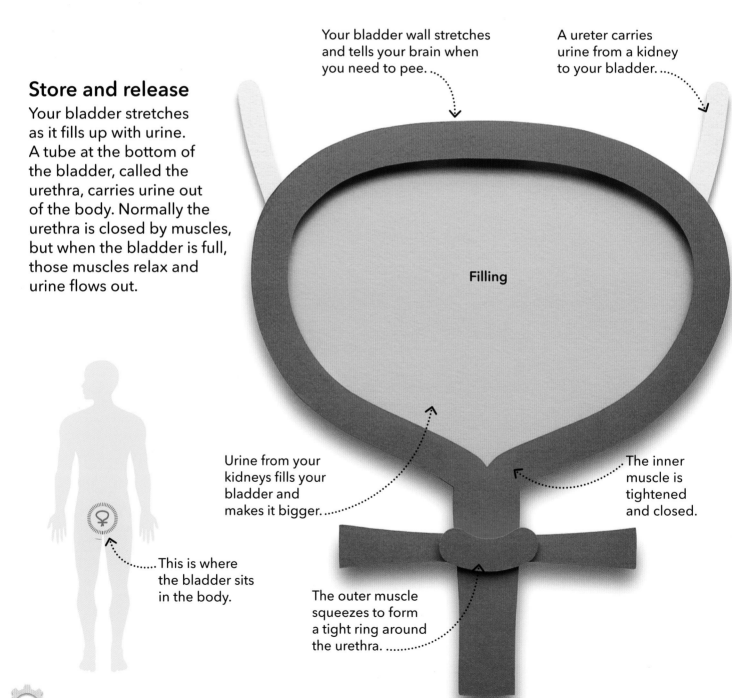

Your bladder wall stretches and tells your brain when you need to pee.

A ureter carries urine from a kidney to your bladder.

Filling

Urine from your kidneys fills your bladder and makes it bigger.

The inner muscle is tightened and closed.

This is where the bladder sits in the body.

The outer muscle squeezes to form a tight ring around the urethra.

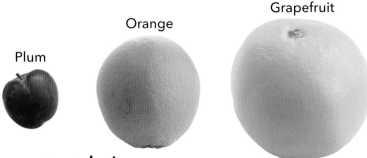

Plum

Orange

Grapefruit

## Super stretchy!

Your bladder can get bigger as it fills up because its wall stretches. When empty, it is about the size of a plum. But as the bladder expands it can reach the size of an orange or even a grapefruit. By this time you would really feel the need to pee (urinate).

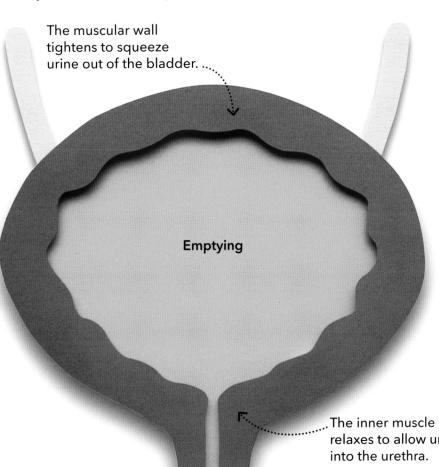

The muscular wall tightens to squeeze urine out of the bladder. ...

Emptying

The inner muscle relaxes to allow urine into the urethra.

The urethra carries urine to the outside of the body. ...

The outer muscle relaxes to let urine flow down the urethra.

## What is urine?

Urine is mostly water. Wastes such as urea, and other substances that the body wants to get rid of, are dissolved in that water.

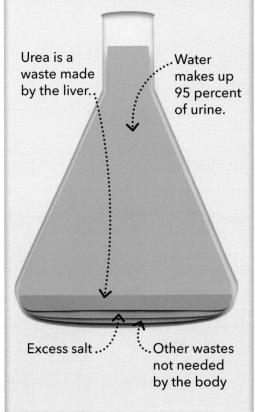

Urea is a waste made by the liver. ...

Water makes up 95 percent of urine.

Excess salt ...

Other wastes not needed by the body

Each year, **a person** releases enough **urine to fill two bathtubs.**

# Water of life

You cannot live without water. It forms an essential part of your cells, tissues, and organs. Without water they just would not work. Your brain controls the amount of water inside your body so that it always stays the same.

Every day your body loses about 2 pints (1 liter) of water—enough water to fill a big **soda bottle!**

## Water balance

Every day your body loses water. You replace that lost water every time you drink or eat. The amount of water you take in and the amount you lose is carefully balanced. While amounts vary depending on exercise and other factors, this diagram gives an idea of how water balance works.

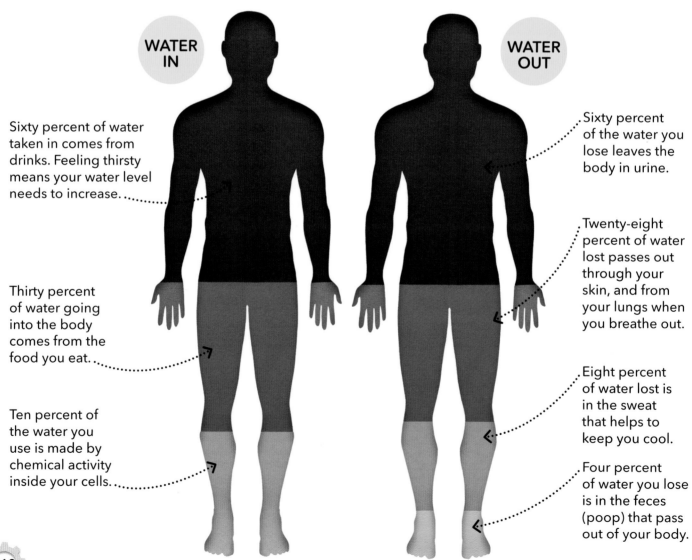

**WATER IN**

**WATER OUT**

Sixty percent of water taken in comes from drinks. Feeling thirsty means your water level needs to increase.

Thirty percent of water going into the body comes from the food you eat.

Ten percent of the water you use is made by chemical activity inside your cells.

Sixty percent of the water you lose leaves the body in urine.

Twenty-eight percent of water lost passes out through your skin, and from your lungs when you breathe out.

Eight percent of water lost is in the sweat that helps to keep you cool.

Four percent of water you lose is in the feces (poop) that pass out of your body.

## How watery are you?

Up to 74 percent, or three-quarters, of a baby's body weight is made up of water. As we get older, the amount of water in the body gets less. However, it still makes up half or more of a young adult's body weight.

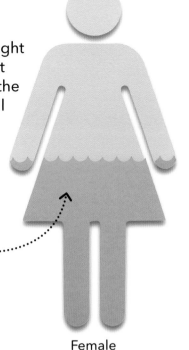

A young woman's body is about 50 percent water. ............

Female

A young man's body is about 60 percent water.

Male

## Work up a sweat!

When you run fast your muscles work really hard. The extra heat they release makes you hot and sweaty. As watery sweat is lost from your skin, it cools you down and keeps your body machine at just the right temperature. But the water you lose as sweat has to be replaced.

## Fluid food

You get the water your body needs from food as well as from drinks. Even the driest crackers contain some water. Fruits and vegetables are especially rich in water. Here are some of the winners in the water league. Cucumber and watermelon are nearly all water!

Cucumber
96% water

Potato
79% water

Watermelon
96% water

Strawberry
92% water

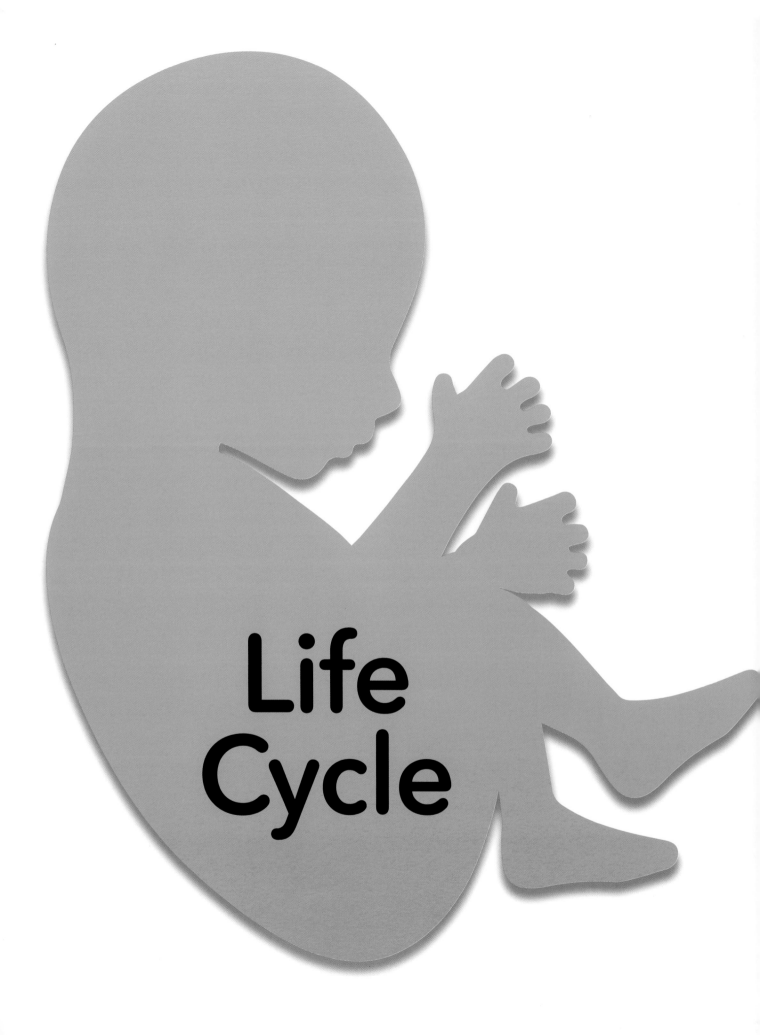

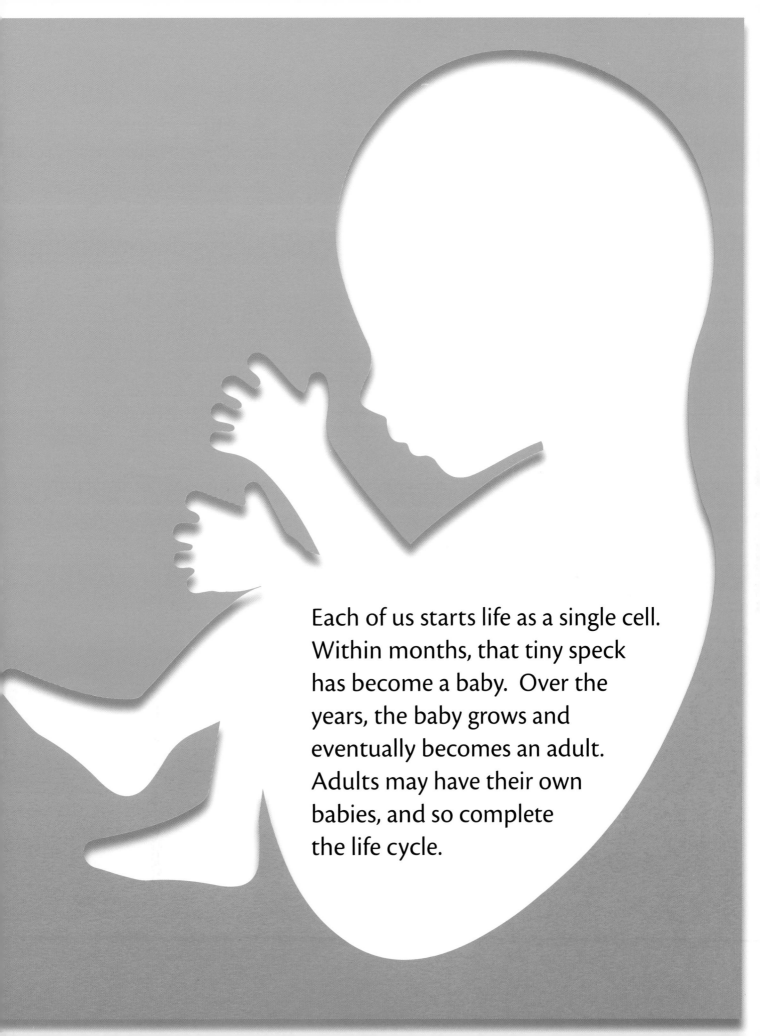

Each of us starts life as a single cell. Within months, that tiny speck has become a baby. Over the years, the baby grows and eventually becomes an adult. Adults may have their own babies, and so complete the life cycle.

# Starting out

To make a baby, the woman provides an egg cell, and the man provides a sperm cell. The way the cells join together is the start of the process that made you and all other humans.

## An egg's journey

Each month, part of a woman's reproductive system, called the ovary, releases an egg that travels to her uterus. If that egg meets a man's sperm on the way, the two join together, in a process called fertilization. The fertilized egg contains all the instructions needed to make a baby.

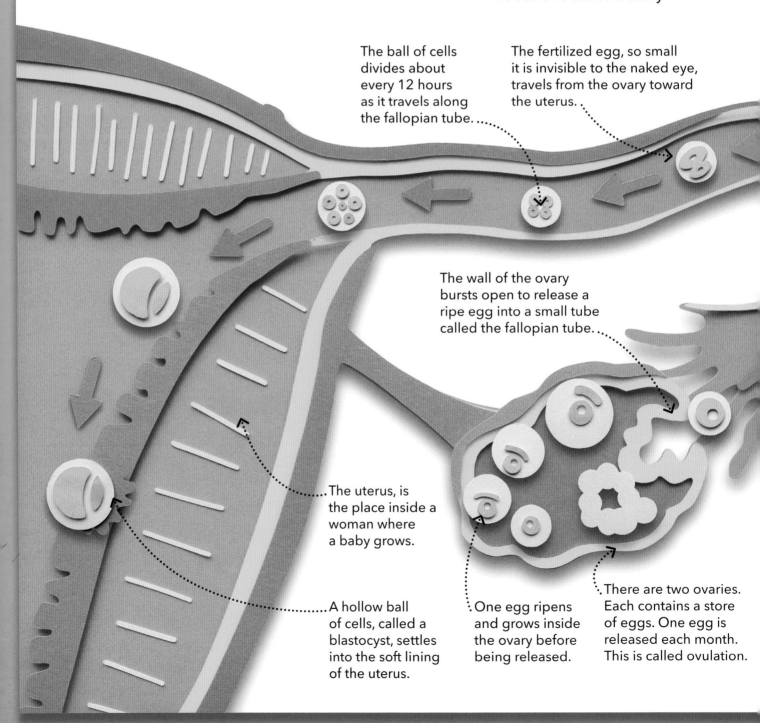

The ball of cells divides about every 12 hours as it travels along the fallopian tube.

The fertilized egg, so small it is invisible to the naked eye, travels from the ovary toward the uterus.

The wall of the ovary bursts open to release a ripe egg into a small tube called the fallopian tube.

The uterus, is the place inside a woman where a baby grows.

A hollow ball of cells, called a blastocyst, settles into the soft lining of the uterus.

One egg ripens and grows inside the ovary before being released.

There are two ovaries. Each contains a store of eggs. One egg is released each month. This is called ovulation.

# Divide and grow

In the days after fertilization, the egg divides again and again. After a week, a hollow ball of cells has formed. Its inner part will develop into the embryo that eventually grows into a baby.

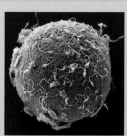

Sperm (blue) surround an egg. Just one sperm enters the egg to fertilize it.

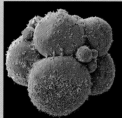

Three days after fertilization, the fertilized egg has divided three times to produce eight cells.

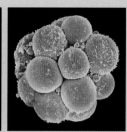

One day later, the cells have divided twice more to form a ball of 16 cells.

Six days after fertilization, a ball of cells has formed. It settles in the uterus.

Sperm swim toward the egg and one sperm fertilizes it. This fertilized cell soon divides into two cells.

The released egg contains half the instructions needed to make a person.

The head contains the package of genetic instructions called DNA.

This middle section supplies the energy needed to move the tail.

The tail beats from side to side to move the sperm forward.

**You and everyone else** started life as a **single cell.**

## Super swimmers

Sperm are unlike any other body cells. They look a little like skinny tadpoles, and millions of them are made every day. They move by beating their tails. Sperm swim toward an egg, carrying half of the instructions needed to make a baby.

# Growing a human

A few days after fertilization happens, a tiny ball of cells settles inside the uterus. Over the next nine months, this ball of cells grows and develops into a new human being. This period of time is called pregnancy. During this time, the growing baby is protected and kept warm within a fluid-filled bag.

## The developing fetus

Before he or she is born, the baby is called an embryo and then a fetus. As the weeks progress, the developing fetus looks increasingly human. A lifeline called the umbilical cord carries vital supplies of food and oxygen from the mother's blood to the fetus.

It takes **21 weeks** for a fetus to grow to the length and weight of a **banana.**

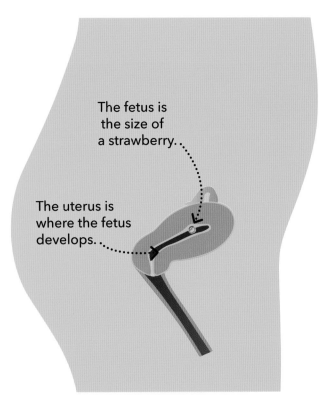

The fetus is the size of a strawberry.

The uterus is where the fetus develops.

The umbilical cord carries food and oxygen to the fetus.

The placenta links the mother's and baby's blood supplies.

**8 weeks**
Eight weeks after fertilization the fetus' main organs are formed. The heart pumps blood, the bones have started to harden, and the arms and legs have grown.

**12 weeks**
Now the size of a lemon, the fetus looks more human, with the eyes closer together. The fetus can make simple arm and hand movements. The kidneys make urine.

## Ultrasound

Doctors can check if a fetus is developing normally with an ultrasound scan. This uses very high-pitched sounds that we cannot hear and which are harmless. Sound waves beamed into a pregnant woman's uterus bounce back as "echoes." These are turned into moving images shown on a screen. The first organ we can generally see in a developing fetus is the beating heart at around 6–8 weeks.

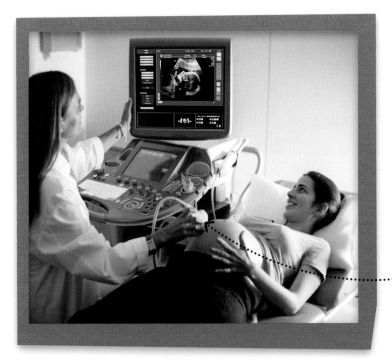

As a probe sends sound waves into a woman's uterus, echoes from her fetus can be seen on the screen.

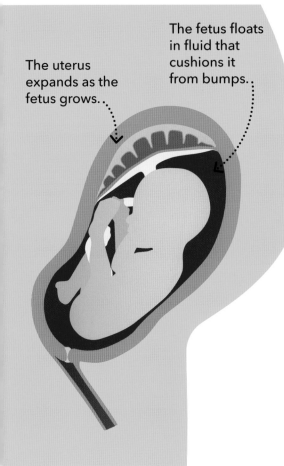

The uterus expands as the fetus grows.

The fetus floats in fluid that cushions it from bumps.

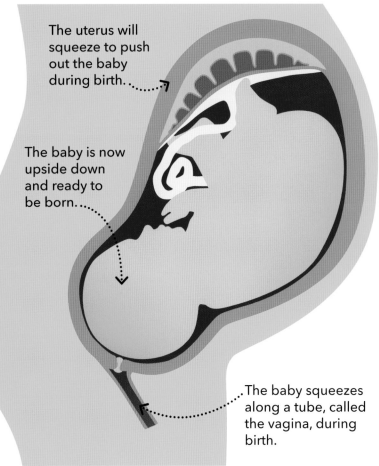

The uterus will squeeze to push out the baby during birth.

The baby is now upside down and ready to be born.

The baby squeezes along a tube, called the vagina, during birth.

### 24 weeks
Over half way through pregnancy, the fetus can yawn and make faces. The fetus responds to sounds and the mother can feel him or her kicking.

### 40 weeks
The fetus is now a fully grown baby. The lungs are well-developed and ready for the baby to take a first breath when he or she emerges into the world.

# Bigger and stronger

After a baby is born, rapid growth takes place and continues for the first two years. Gradually, children become more skilled at moving and thinking. They learn to understand themselves and they make friends. From around 11 onward, a child starts adolescence. A key part of this is puberty, when she or he grows rapidly and her or his body changes shape.

## Child development

Children grow and develop at different rates, but here are some of the important stages from childhood to adolescence.

This girl can balance on one leg.

This boy has the skills to learn a musical instrument.

This girl is very active and playful.

**5 years old**
This child is over half her adult height. She can have a conversation and is starting to read and write. She can run, jump, and kick a ball.

**6 years old**
This boy can sing, tell stories, ride a bike, read simple books, and write his own name. He enjoys playing with his friends.

**9 years old**
This child can hold her balance. She can play sports and dance. She thinks carefully about things. She makes strong friendships.

A two year-old picks up **10 or more new words** each day.

..........This boy is strong, more self-aware, and independent.

.....Muscles develop further

**11 years upward**

This boy is now approaching adolescence and about to become an adult. He can speak and write well, and has a good memory. He can participate in team sports.

# Changing shape

When you were a baby, your head was large in proportion to the rest of your body. That is because at first, the brain grows and develops very quickly. During childhood, the rest of your body gradually catches up, so that by the time you are a teenager your body proportions look much more like an adult's.

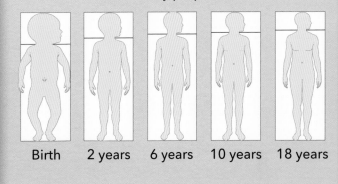

### Head-body proportions

| Birth | 2 years | 6 years | 10 years | 18 years |

## Puberty

Around the ages of 10–12 in girls and 12–14 in boys, the body grows and develops rapidly. The reproductive system also starts working. This stage is called puberty. One sign of puberty in a boy is growing facial hair, so he needs to start shaving.

# Growing older

People change as they grow. Children develop and become teenagers. They then turn into young adults. Over time, people grow older. The body gradually slows down as it starts to wear out. The cells in the body do not divide so well, and other cells tend to die, making us a bit wrinkled and old looking.

## Four women

Here are four women from different generations of the same family: a daughter, mother, grandmother, and great-grandmother. They show the changes that happen to the body as people get older.

**Teenager**
This girl is nearly fully grown. The period of change and development from childhood to adulthood is called adolescence.

**Thirties**
This woman's body has stopped growing. She has had a child. The woman is strong, healthy, and active.

**Fifties**
This woman shows signs of aging, with stiffer joints and weaker muscles. Diet and exercise help her stay healthy.

## Wrinkles

People's skin naturally becomes wrinklier as they get older. The skin is thinner and drier than in younger people. There are also fewer of the tiny fibers in skin that give it both firmness and springiness. All these things combine to make wrinkles happen.

With aging, hair turns gray or white. This is because it loses a substance called melanin, which gives hair its color.

This X-ray of the hand of an older person with arthritis shows the finger bones bent to one side.

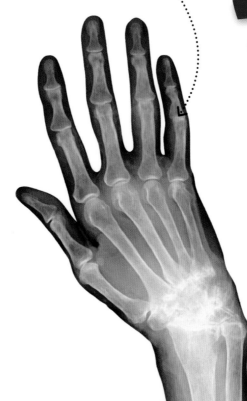

Jeanne Calment from France **lived until she was 122** and is the oldest known human.

## Stiff joints

People can become stiffer as they get older. Some people suffer from arthritis. This is a disease that affects the joints between bones, often in the hands, hips, and knees. Joints swell and become painful, making movement difficult. As this X-ray shows, arthritis can also push bones out of position.

**Seventies**
This woman's muscles and bones are weaker. But she does gentle exercise to keep healthy and enjoy life.

# Glossary

**artery**
Tube carrying blood rich in oxygen from the heart to the tissues

**atrium**
One of two chambers of the heart receiving blood from the lungs or elsewhere in the body

**bacteria**
Tiny living things, mostly helpful for health. Some cause disease, such as food poisoning or a sore throat

**base**
One of four key parts of DNA. Like letters in words, they can be put together to spell out instructions that control cells

**bile**
Fluid made in the liver and stored in the gall bladder, containing enzymes important for digestion

**calcium**
Mineral element found in many foods, including milk and vegetables. Calcium helps build bones, nails, and teeth

**capillary**
Tiny blood vessel carrying blood through the tissues from arteries to veins

**carbohydrate**
Substance, such as sugar or starch, that supplies energy

**carbon dioxide**
Gas given off by the body's cells as they consume energy. It is breathed out from the lungs

**cartilage**
Tough, flexible tissue in the nose, ears, ends of bones, and ribs. It helps the smooth, frictionless movement of joints

**cell**
One of the trillions of microscopic, living units that are the building blocks of the human body. Together, they form tissues

**cerebrum**
Part of the brain involved in activities such as thinking, memory, movement, and sensation

**cochlea**
Tubular structure deep in the ear that detects vibrations made from sound waves, converting them into electrical signals for the brain

**chromosomes**
One of 23 strands of DNA in a cell's nucleus, with most of the instructions needed to run the cell

**dermis**
Thick underlayer in the skin, containing blood vessels, sweat glands, and nerve endings

**diaphragm**
Big muscle separating the chest from the abdomen. Its role is to help breathing

**digestion**
Process in the stomach and bowel that breaks food up into smaller components for nutrition

**DNA**
Substance formed of two twisted strands, present in each chromosome

**embryo**
Earliest stage of a baby's development, before its organs are fully formed

**enamel**
Hardest part of the outside of a tooth

**endocrine gland**
Organ that releases hormones directly into the bloodstream

**enzymes**
Substances that speed up the breakdown of nutrients in digestion

**epidermis**
Thin, outer layer of skin

**fat**
Fat in foods is a source of energy. The body's fat cells also give it its shape and insulate it

**feces**
Solid waste left after food is digested. It also contains dead cells and bacteria

**fertilization**
When the egg and sperm join to produce an embryo

**fetus**
The developing baby inside the womb

**gene**
Parts of the DNA forming coded instructions to control different cells

**germ**
Tiny bodies, such as bacteria or viruses, which often cause diseases

**gland**
Organ that releases useful substances into the body, for example, the salivary glands that make saliva

**glucose**
Type of sugar that is an important source of energy for all cells

**hormone**
Substance that acts as a chemical message, controlling the activity of some cells

**immune system**
Bone marrow, white cells, thymus, spleen, and other organs that defend the body against foreign molecules and germs

**intestine**
Tube running from the end of the stomach to the anus

**joint**
Part of the skeleton where bones meet, which helps with movement

**liver**
The largest organ, which is important in filtering blood, dealing with waste and toxins, and helping digestion

**lymph**
Fluid from the immune system containing white blood cells, including lymphocytes. It circulates in lymph vessels (lymphatics)

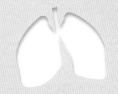    

**macrophage**
Specialized white cell that engulfs foreign particles and germs

**metabolism**
Chemical processes responsible, for example, for energy production and digestion

**mineral**
Substance, such as calcium or iron, needed in small amounts for health

**mitochondrion**
Tiny complex body inside cells that releases energy

**muscle fiber**
Long cell that shortens by contraction when muscles work

**nerve**
Long string of neurons, carrying impulses between the brain, the spinal cord, and parts of the body

**neuron**
Nerve cell

**nutrient**
Substance, such as protein, fat, or a vitamin, needed to provide essential fuel for growth and function

**organ**
Structure in the body made of specialized cells, such as the heart, kidney, stomach, or lung

**organelle**
Tiny structure in cells, such as a mitochondrion

**oxygen**
Gas in the atmosphere that supports life. It plays a vital part in energy metabolism

**papilla**
Tiny bumps on the tongue that detect taste

**peristalsis**
Waves of muscle relaxation and contraction, pushing food, cells, or fluid through various tubes in the body

**plasma**
Liquid containing blood cells, which forms the blood. It carries nutrients, hormones, and waste products.

**protein**
Essential part of a person's diet, found in meat, fish, eggs, and nuts. Proteins promote growth and build most of the body's tissues, including muscle

**puberty**
A time when changes occur in the body as a child starts to develop into a young adult

**receptor**
Part of a cell that receives and detects chemical signals, often from another cell

**skeletal muscle**
Type of muscle, found in the legs, arms, face, and chest, which helps you move. It is usually controlled voluntarily

**smooth muscle**
Type of muscle in many organs, including your bowel, blood vessels, and bladder, over which there is limited or no voluntary control

**spleen**
Organ near the stomach that makes blood cells and helps the immune system

**synapse**
Tiny gap between neurons, across which chemical signals pass. Brain cells have thousands of these connections

**system**
Group of linked organs working together. For example, the kidneys and bladder form the urinary system

**tendon**
Toughened connective tissue that connects muscles to bone

**thymus**
Organ in the chest, most active in children, making the cells of the immune system

**tissue**
Group of cells that function together

**toxin**
Substance that is harmful. Some bacteria release toxins

**trillion**
One million million (1,000,000,000,000)

**ultrasound**
High-pitched sound waves, undetectable by the human ear. Ultrasound echoes are used to create images of structures deep inside the body

**urine**
Watery waste made by the kidneys and stored in the bladder before being released

**vein**
Blood vessel carrying blood from the tissues toward the heart

**ventricle**
One of two muscular pumping chambers of the heart

**vertebra**
One of the small bones, running from the neck to the pelvis, which are linked to form the backbone

**virus**
Tiny, germ-invading cells. Viruses cause illnesses, including flu and chicken pox, but most viruses in the body are harmless

**vitamin**
One of around 13 substances, including vitamins A and C, needed in small amounts in food to ensure that the body stays healthy

**X-ray**
Radiation used to create shadows of bones and other organs in the body. Images on an X-ray photo can reveal internal damage and disease

# Index

# Acknowledgments

Dorling Kindersley would like to thank the following people for their assistance in the preparation of this book: Helen Peters for the index; Polly Goodman for proofreading; Cecile Landau for editorial assistance; Clare Joyce and Molly Lattin for additional design.

**Picture Credits:**
The publisher would also like to thank the following for their kind permission to reproduce their photographs:

(Key: a-above; b-below/bottom; c-center; f-far; l-left; r-right; t-top)

**123RF.com**: parinya binsuk / parinyabinsuk 89tl; Anna Grigorjeva / candy18 48; pat138241 119cr; Alexander Raths / alexraths 121tc; Oksana Tkachuk / ksena32 88br; Andrii Vergeles / vixit 65cr. **Alamy Stock Photo**: Olaf Doering 107br; David Ponton / Design Pics Inc 49tr; WILDLIFE GmbH 88-89b. **Dorling Kindersley**: Sarah Ashun 103fcla; Neil Fletcher 88cb; Tim Parmenter / Natural History Museum 21bc; Martin Richardson / Rough Guides 50clb; 50bl. **Dreamstime.com**: Exopixel 119crb; Rawpixelimages 12-13; Tetiana Zbrodko / Taratata 88fbl.

**Fotolia**: Flying Wizard 49c; Zee 88cr. **Getty Images**: Francesco Buresta / EyeEm 43br; Corbis / VCG 117tl; FatCamera / E+ 111cl; Steve Gschmeissner / SPL / Science Photo Library 97cr; Image Source 11bl; Image Source / DigitalVision 32-33; Jose Luis Pelaez Inc / Blend Images 120-121; Rubberball / Chris Alvanas 118cb; Science Photo Library 59br, 78bl; Science Photo Library - Miriam Maslo 121bc; Science Photo Library - Steve Gschmeissner / Brand X Pictures 99bc. **David Peart**: 75tr. **Science Photo Library**: 11tc, 35bc, 67br; AMI Images / NIAID 84cl; Juergen Berger 85bl; Dr. Tony Brain 85tl; Pr. Michel Brauner / ISM 25bc; Scott Camazine, Sue Trainor 28-29; Thomas Deerinck, NCMIR 43bc; Eye of Science 115tl; GJLP 31cr; Steve Gschmeissner 15tr, 15ca, 53tr; Ted Kinsman 15tc, 27tl; Leonard Lessin 51tr, 51cra; Maximilian Stock Ltd 102-103; Microscape 35bl, 35fbl; Prof. P. Motta / Dept. of Anatomy / University "La Sapienza", Rome 26bl; National Cancer Institute 64-65; Dr. Yorgos Nikas 115tc, 115tr, 115ftr; Susumu Nishinaga 107tl; Martin Oeggerli 37tr; David M. Phillips 15crb; Power and Syred 15cra; David Scharf 18clb, 88tr; Sovereign, ISM 47cr, 47crb; Richard Wehr / Custom Medical Stock Photo 83bc; Zephyr 45tr.

All other images © Dorling Kindersley
For further information see: www.dkimages.com